Dark Times.
Broken People.
FAITHFUL KING.

Donna Gaines
Marge Lenow
Jean Stockdale
Dayna Street
Angie Wilson

Dark Times. Broken People. Faithful King

©2019 Bellevue Baptist Church

All rights reserved. No part of this publication may be reproduced, stored in a retrieval system or transmitted in any form by any means, electronic, mechanical, photocopy, recording, or otherwise, without the prior permission of the author, except as provided for by USA copyright law.

Cover and book design: Amanda Weaver
Chart and Map: Lauren Gooden
Editing: Dayna Street, Donita Barnwell, Melissa Bobo Hardee, Lauren Gooden, Vera Sidhom

Unless otherwise indicated, Scripture taken from the NEW AMERICAN STANDARD BIBLE.® Copyright © 1960, 1962, 1963, 1968, 1971, 1973, 1975, 1977, 1995 by Lockman Foundation. Used by permission. www.Lockman.org

CONTENTS

How to Use This Study 5

Map of Israel during Judges 7

Timeline 9

Chart of the Judges 11

Introduction – Dark Times. Broken People. Faithful King 13

Week 1 – When You Forget 19

Week 2 – When You Live With Idols 35

Week 3 – When an Ezer Leads 55

Week 4 – When You Triumph Over Fear 77

Week 5 – When You Win the Battle But Lose the War 97

Week 6 – When Power Goes to Your Head 119

Week 7 – When You Think Before You Speak 137

Week 8 – When the Weak Becomes Strong 161

Week 9 – When the Strong Becomes Weak 181

Week 10 – When You Thought Things Couldn't Get Worse 197

How To Use This Study

Imagine a nation struggling as everyone does what is right in his or her own eyes. Envision a culture disintegrating as the erosion of morality plummets it into a downward spiral of depravity. Picture a people falling into hopelessness as they are repeatedly broken and enslaved by sin. These dark times depicted in the book of Judges sound familiar, don't they? The post-Christian world we live in increasingly mirrors this desperate time in Israel's history.

But there is hope! We have a Faithful KING who never fails to redeem those who call upon Him. *Dark Times. Broken People. FAITHFUL KING.* is a ten-week study in the book of Judges that traces the hand of God in Israel's history and gives us hope for today (and the future) as we discover and apply timely truths based upon His Word.

This study is designed to provide an opportunity for personal study throughout the week leading up to a small group discussion and large group teaching time once a week. Each session is divided into five daily homework assignments that provide Bible study and personal application.

In your small group time each week, you will be able to connect with other women and build life-giving, sharpening relationships. As you meet together, be ready to share what God has shown you through His Word using the weekly studies as a guide. In the large group teaching time, you will be challenged by relevant, biblical instruction that will encourage you to stand firm on the truth of God's Word.

As we have written this study, our hearts have overflowed with thanksgiving to God for His unconditional faithfulness and love toward us. Our prayer is that your journey through Judges will cause you to have the same worship-filled response.

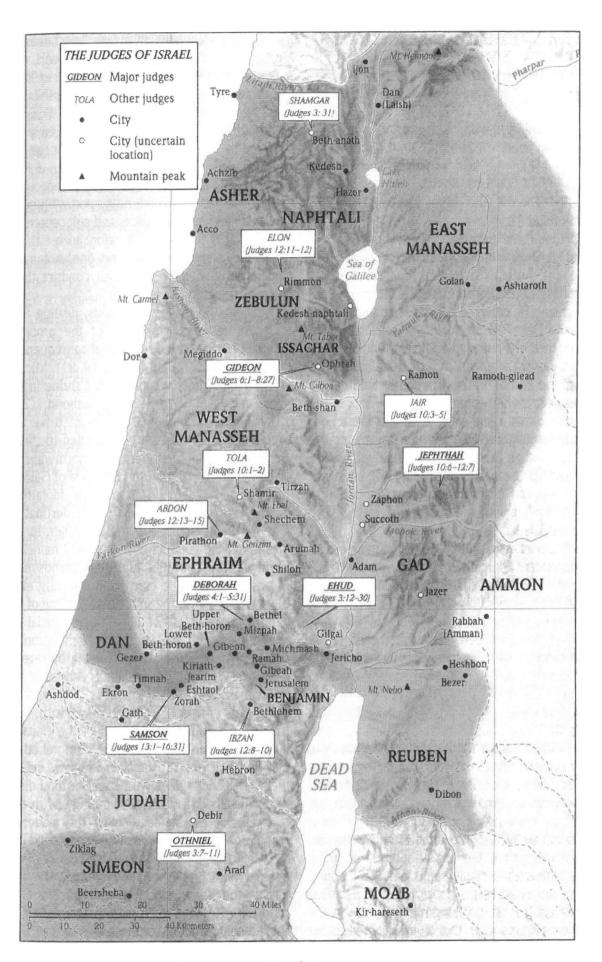

Map | 7

Judges in the Old Testament Timeline

Date	Biblical Books	Significant Events
Creation	GENESIS	• Creation of the world, fall of mankind • Time of the patriarchs • Israel is enslaved to Egypt for 400 years
1446 BC	EXODUS LEVITICUS NUMBERS	• Moses leads Israel out of Egypt • Giving of the law
1406 BC	DEUTERONOMY JOSHUA	• Moses dies • Joshua begins conquest of Promised Land
1380 BC	JUDGES RUTH	• Joshua dies • Time of the judges
1000 BC	SAMUEL KINGS CHRONICLES	• Saul becomes Israel's first king • By 500 BC, monarchy ends and people are in exile

The Judges of Israel (in Judges)

Judge	Tribe	Oppressed by	# of Years Oppressed	# of Years Ruled	Notable Facts	Scripture References
Othniel	*Judah*	*Mesopotamians*	*8*	*40*	*The Spirit of the Lord came upon him*	Judges 1:9-21; 3:1-11
Ehud						Judges 3:12-30
Shamgar						Judges 3:31
Deborah						Judges 4:1-5:31
Gideon						Judges 6:1-8:32
Tola						Judges 10:1-2
Jair						Judges 10:3-4
Jephthah						Judges 10:6-12:7
Ibzan						Judges 12:8-10
Elon						Judges 12:11-12
Abdon						Judges 12:13-15
Samson						Judges 13:1-16:31

Dark Times. Broken People. Faithful KING.
Introduction

But I assure you of this: If you ever forget the LORD your God...you will certainly be destroyed.
Deuteronomy 8:19 (NLT)

What happens when we forget God?

It may surprise you to learn that Russia was at one time considered among the most Christian nations in the world–a land "pregnant with spiritual heritage and strongly in touch with the oldest traditions of the faith."[1] How is it that such a nation became the first state in the world where atheism became an official ideology?

For several centuries, Russia was steeped in an Orthodox Christianity, which remained true to the tenets of the early church. Piety was more important than fame or riches and faith was the unifying force that shaped the nation. But in the late 19th century, things began to change. Secularism and indifference began to infiltrate the church. The Marxist belief that morality was relative, not absolute, was sweeping the nation, a belief that was increasingly embraced by the clergy, who were not always models of veneration.[2] By the time of the Bolshevik Revolution in 1917, personal faith had virtually disappeared from Russian educated circles; and even among the uneducated peasantry, its existence was diminishing.

By 1922, Lenin had stripped churches of their monetary valuables in order to fund his Red Army and in the ensuing years under Stalin and Khruschchev, thousands of churches were torn down, leaving entire cities and districts without a church.[3] Under Stalin's regime alone, the persecution unleashed upon the Russian people by a "murderous state atheism, coupled with the corroding effect of its lies"[4] led to the deaths of millions.

In 1975, Aleksandr Solzhenitsyn, a Russian novelist who was imprisoned, sentenced to forced labor in the gulag, and then expelled from the country, reflected on the tragedies that had consumed his country during the twentieth century:

> More than half a century ago, while I was still a child, I recall hearing a number of older people offer the following explanation for the great disasters that had befallen Russia: "Men have forgotten God; that's why all this has happened."

> Since then I have spent well-nigh 50 years working on the history of our Revolution; in the process I have read hundreds of books, collected hundreds of personal testimonies, and have already contributed eight volumes of my own toward the effort of clearing away the rubble left by that

upheaval. But if I were asked today to formulate as concisely as possible the main cause of the ruinous Revolution that swallowed up some 60 million of our people, I could not put it more accurately than to repeat: "Men have forgotten God; that's why all this has happened."⁵

Whether spiritual amnesia penetrates the heart of an individual or permeates the soul of an entire nation, the outcome is always catastrophic.

Men have forgotten God. Whether spiritual amnesia penetrates the heart of an individual or permeates the soul of an entire nation, the outcome is always catastrophic. What happened in Russia in the twentieth century is a case of history repeating itself. The great disasters that fell upon Israel during the period of the Judges find their roots in this same tragic soil. They forgot God.

The account of Israel in the book of Judges is the story of a nation that begins with a great spiritual heritage. "The people served the Lord all the days of Joshua, and all the days of the elders who survived Joshua, who had seen all the great work of the Lord which He had done for Israel" (Judges 2:7). And then the gravitational pull of sin sucked the nation into a downward spiral and "The sons of Israel did what was evil in the sight of the Lord, and forgot the Lord their God..." (Judges 3:7).

Why? What were they thinking? How could that happen?

As we interact with God's Word throughout this study, we will discover the answers to these questions. But first, let's address some of the FAQs (Frequently Asked Questions) about the book of Judges as we paint the backdrop for this historical narrative.

FAQs about Judges

Who wrote the book?

Judges gives no hint of the identity of the author. Jewish tradition attributes the authorship to the prophet Samuel who served as the last judge of Israel, but no one knows for sure who the human writer of Judges was. However, we can be confident that the author of all Scripture is the Holy Spirit of God. Peter writes, "But know this first of all, that no prophecy of Scripture is a matter of one's own interpretation, for no prophecy was ever made by an act of human will, but men moved by the Holy Spirit spoke from God" (2 Peter 1:20-21). Paul adds, "All Scripture is inspired by God and profitable for teaching, for reproof, for correction, for training in righteousness" (2 Timothy 3:16).

When was it written?

Most theologians believe that Judges was written during the period of the kings.⁶ We know that the time of the writing was earlier than David's capture of Jerusalem in 2 Samuel 5:6-7 since the Jebusites still controlled the city (Judges 1:21). Also, the author writes about a time before a king ruled Israel (Judges 17:6; 18:1; 21:25). Judges was possibly written during Saul's reign that began around 1051 B.C.⁷

Introduction | 14

Why was it written?
Judges has a three-fold message. **First**, the consequences of sin always cost us more than we think they will. Judges records the story of a nation "that turned away from its grand heritage to reap a grim harvest." [8] **Second**, people are unfaithful, but God is faithful. Over and over, God rescues Israel in spite of Israel. **Third**, Judges was written to look forward to a righteous King, Jesus. Judges plants the seeds of future messianic hope by showing us how the Israelites atrophied in their sin without such a King.

What is the setting?
The book of Judges acts as the sequel to the book of Joshua, linked by similar accounts of Joshua's death (Joshua 24:29-31; Judges 2:6-9). The events that occur within the book of Judges span the geographical expanse of the nation of Israel, happening in a variety of cities, towns, and battlefields.

Chronologically, Judges is the second historical book of the Bible. It covers the period of time between the death of Joshua and the beginning of the monarchy of Saul. If the judges ruled consecutively, the book would cover 390 years since the number of years each judge served is given. However, as there was no central ruling authority during the time, the judges were actually regional rulers and some judges ruled simultaneously making it difficult to nail down an exact time period for the setting of the book.[9] The most common guesstimate among commentaries is that the time of the judges spanned around three centuries, a period that covers approximately one-third of the total Old Testament history of Israel.[10]

What is the role of a judge?
The central characters of this chronicle are "judges," a term that refers to the leaders Israel had from the time of the elders who outlived Joshua until the time of the monarchy. The judges were not legal authorities as the modern day word implies. They were military leaders whom God empowered to rescue His people, "Then the Lord raised up judges who delivered them from the hands of those who plundered them" (Judges 2:16). After the military threat was over, the judges continued in leadership roles, but none of them established an empire.

Major Themes in Judges

Dark Times
At the time of the book of Judges, the Israelites have experienced God's deliverance from the bondage of Egypt. He has guided them providentially through the wilderness, and He has given them the Promised Land–Canaan. And yet, they have forgotten Him. It is as if the light grew dim for Israel when Joshua died and darkness descended upon the nation as the elders who led after Joshua also died. The next generation "did not know the Lord, nor yet the work which He had done for them" (Judges 2:10).

Evidently, in the space of just a few decades, the Israelites lost sight of a basic principle of spiritual transference: to train their children in the ways of the Lord (Proverbs 22:6). Moses had instructed the parents of Israel to teach their children the narrative of their miraculous story of redemption and the content of God's covenant with His people

(Deuteronomy 6:7-9). Over and over, their history revealed God's love and provision, a history that would fortify their faith in the Promised Land. But. Each generation would need to be continually reminded of His mighty works on their behalf or else they would risk the awareness of God's faithfulness vanishing from the collective conscience of the nation. Tragically, that is exactly what happened.

Broken People

The inevitable result of forgetting God is sin. And in the book of Judges, we see the cycle of sin repeated with increasing depravity. Sadly, the sins of the culture become the sins of God's people as the lifestyles of their pagan neighbors shout louder than the whispers of their fading convictions. The people are broken. The nation is a mess. And the scenario just keeps on repeating itself.

Faithful KING

The people forgot their God, but God does not forget them. The Psalmist sums up God's faithful thoughts toward His faithless people, "Yet He was merciful; He forgave their iniquities and did not destroy them. Time after time He restrained his anger and did not stir up His full wrath" (Psalm 78:38, NIV). Generation after generation, the Israelites sin. Time after time, God chastens them. Over and over, God raises up a judge to rescue His people. But when that judge dies, the sinful state of the nation spirals downward.

This repetitive cycle reveals that what Israel needs, what mankind needs, is a King. One who will reign eternally and deliver us from the bondage of our sin. The King of Kings. The perfect Deliverer. His name is Jesus. Our Faithful KING.

Judges for the 21st Century

We are living in dark times in America, days much like those depicted in Judges. Days very similar to the times in late 19th century Russia. It is not that we have completely forgotten God, but we are teetering on a dangerous precipice.

The writer of Judges communicates more clearly that things formerly thought to happen only among the pagan Canaanites began occurring in Israel. The familiar refrain, "Everyone did what was right in his own eyes" provides not only a synopsis of the conditions in Ancient Israel, but it is also is an ominous summary of 21st century American thought. Same-sex marriage, abortion, sexual abuse, and the sex trafficking of children are all symptoms of a nation that has succumbed to "Canaanization" at its core. A century ago, no one would have imagined these atrocities occurring on our streets. Today, no one is surprised.

As believers, we must wake up, stand up, and speak up and allow the present darkness among us be a rallying call to action. Let us shake off our spiritual amnesia, repent, and seek God for revival. Within ourselves. In our church. Throughout our nation.

Let us not forget God, but remember to do what is right in His eyes, not our own.

I have heard all about you, LORD. I am filled with awe by your amazing works. In this time of our deep need, help us again as you did in years gone by. And in your anger, remember your mercy.
Habakkuk 3:2, NLT

WEEK 1

When You Forget
Judges 1-2

The most shocking feature in the book of Judges…is not the horror of the people's sin depicted in these narratives but the glory of salvation from that sin accomplished by the God of patience, mercy, compassion, steadfast love, and faithfulness (Exodus 34:6).[1]
~J. I. Packer

The book of Judges is a modern day commentary on our culture. Even though we are 3,000 years removed from their day, we see the behavior and circumstances of the Israelites being replicated in our own time. As we begin our study, we find that the people of God, the nation of Israel, are on the brink of a national disaster because they have forgotten their God. Instead of shaping the culture of the land God has given them, they are profoundly influenced by the pagan nations and idolatry around them.

Certainly, we are shocked at the depravity and the faulty reasoning of God's people. And yet, we can see within the modern day church the very same thing happening when we elevate our reasoning above God's Word. We sense the division among God's people today as we lean on our own natural reasoning instead of what God has revealed through Scripture. When we stop trusting God as THE source of truth and morality, we lose our influence and end up looking and acting like the people around us. Just like the dark times of the Judges.

When we stop trusting God as THE source of truth and morality, we lose our influence and end up looking and acting like the people around us.

As Dr. Julie Slattery notes in her book, *Rethinking Sexuality*,

> Although this is a modern problem, it is not a new problem. The Bible tells us that even thousands of years ago, people thought they knew better than God. One ancient example is the condition of Israel during the time of the judges…This Old Testament book describes a crazy period in Israel's history, a time of sexual confusion much like our own. The nation of Israel had a spiritual heritage and spiritual leaders, but their love for God was mixed with pagan worship and secular thinking.[2]

Consequently, we find ourselves experiencing the societal deterioration that Paul describes in Romans 1. Our culture has by and large rejected the God of creation and is instead worshiping the creature. When that happens, God will give us over to ourselves and the sin we fall headlong into, while we encourage others to join us! This downward spiral of depravity ultimately leads to self-destruction (Romans 1:18-32).

Tim Keller gives a fitting diagnosis of modern day America, "We live and work among a great variety of gods – not only those of other formal religions, but also the gods of wealth, celebrity, pleasure, ideology, achievement. Our era can be characterized by the phrase which sums up the book of Judges: 'Everyone did what was right in his own eyes' (Judges 21:25, ESV)."[3]

WEEK 1 » DAY ONE » OVERVIEW

As we begin our study in Judges this week, we are going to read the book in its entirety to get a general overview. Because you will be reading through the complete book, this week's commentary and questions will not be as involved as future weeks when you will be looking at specific passages. As you read through the twenty-one chapters of Judges, note repeated words or themes and the sin cycle you will see recurring throughout. Pay attention to the judges the Lord raises up as well as the number of years the Israelites live in peace before the death of each judge. Witness the nation's inevitable return to idolatry and subsequent oppression by a pagan people. We will see this cycle repeated seven times.

I found it helpful to note the sin cycle in the margin of my Bible each time it was mentioned. As you read, I will also be asking you to underline specific components of the sin cycle. The goal is for you to interact with the text and notice themes. This study will not be one that spoon-feeds you. We want you to ask questions, make observations, and respond to the Lord as you dig into His Word. God's Word is living and active (Hebrews 4:12). It is God-breathed, and it is still breathing (2 Timothy 3:16).

You will find a double introduction in Judges 1 & 2. Then you will move into the description of Israel's behavior and the judges that God grants them for deliverance. Pay special attention to God's commands to take the land and each specific tribe's obedience or disobedience.

Read Judges 1-10.

1. As you read today, underline the following information in your Bible:

    - Number of years of Israel's oppression

    - Names of the judges

    - Number of years of Israel's peace

2. To whom was the book written?

3. When was the book written? (If you have not already read the Introduction, this is a good time to do so.)

4. Write down the names of the judges who ruled during Judges 1-10.

As you read these chapters, you will find that the judges God raises up become increasingly weak. God uses a variety of people. It is not the person's ability that makes them useful, but their surrender and obedience to God's call. God is in charge and even though His Word is never mentioned in Judges, He is moving and active throughout. God has always worked out His will through flawed people. Our inability to obey and our propensity to lean on our own understanding point us to our need for a Savior.

WEEK 1 » DAY TWO » OVERVIEW

Read Judges 11-16.

1. As you read today, underline the following information in your Bible:
   - Number of years of Israel's oppression
   - Names of the judges
   - Number of years of Israel's peace

2. Which judges led Israel during this period?

3. How many chapters does the writer devote to Samson?

4. What words describe Samson's leadership?

Samson assumes that God will continue to bless him regardless of how many times he gives in to his weaknesses.

5. How do we see this same attitude in our Christian culture or even in our own lives?

As you close your time in God's Word today, reflect on these words written by theologian and martyr, Dietrich Bonhoeffer on temptation:

> In our members there is a slumbering inclination toward desire, which is both sudden and fierce. With irresistible power, desire seizes mastery of the flesh. All at once a secret, smoldering fire is kindled. The flesh burns and is in flames. It makes no difference whether it is a sexual desire, or ambition, or vanity, or desire for revenge, our love of fame and power, or greed for money, or finally, that strange desire for the beauty of the world, of nature. Joy in God is…extinguished in us and we seek all our joy in the creature. At this moment God is quite unreal to us. He loses all reality, and only desire for the creature is real; the only reality is the devil. Satan does not here fill us with hatred of God, but with **forgetfulness of God**. And now his falsehood is added to this proof of strength. The lust thus aroused envelopes the mind and will of a man in deepest darkness. The powers of clear discrimination and of decision are taken from us. The questions present themselves: Is what the flesh desires really sin in this case?" And, "Is it really not permitted me, yes, expected of me now, here in my particular situation to appease desire?"[4]

Do you not know that when you present yourselves to someone as slaves for obedience, you are slaves of the one whom you obey, either of sin resulting in death, or of obedience resulting in righteousness?
Romans 6:16

WEEK 1 » DAY THREE » OVERVIEW

Read Judges 17-21.

1. Write a 2-3 sentence summary of these chapters.

Just as the writer of Judges included a double introduction, we now have a double conclusion. As you read, you will note that there are no judges mentioned in these chapters. The previous chapters give us the facts about the judges and Israel's deliverance. These chapters give us an idea of "what life was like when Israel was left to their own resources. This view of humanity without God is so bleak that these passages are almost never preached upon or even studied."[5]

2. What words describe Micah in chapters 17-18?

The opening words of 19:1 warn us that Israel is continuing to do what is right in their own eyes and evil in the eyes of the Lord. It is heartbreaking to realize that this narrative revolves around a Levite. When sin abounds and people do what is right in their own eyes, women and the vulnerable are always mistreated and undervalued.

3. How does this Levite disregard God's design for marriage?

4. How does the Levite show disregard for the woman?

5. Where do they stop to spend the night and why is this significant?

6. What does the Ephraimite offer the vile men of the city and what does this tell you about this culture's value of women?

As we will consider in more detail later, what is happening here in Gibeah is very similar to what happened in Sodom and Gomorrah in Genesis 19. But these are God's people who had received the covenant given to Abraham and the law delivered to Moses. Yet, they are just like the pagan nations around them who had not received these great blessings and revelation. They have become like Sodom.

How should we react to the events recorded here? We should grieve and mourn. Just as we should about the way women are treated today in the pornography industry, through human trafficking, and through prostitution as well as how the vulnerable are treated through abortion. Our own sins, as those who have received the message of the cross, are reprehensible. You may not have committed any of these sins, but what are you doing to prevent them? One of the most important things we can do is to pray and cry out to the Lord about the sins of our nation.

We can pray 2 Chronicles 7:14 and ask the Lord to awaken the church to our own sin! It is as we repent and turn back to obedience that the Lord "will hear from heaven, will forgive their sin and will heal their land." Did you see that? When His people repent and return, the Lord will heal the land. It will be after our repentance that the eyes of the lost will be opened and many will come to Christ.

As we see the downward spiral of Israel into what appears to be almost total depravity, we are warned about what will happen when we no longer know or obey the commands of God. One of the best descriptions of how we are to live and pass on our faith is recorded in Deuteronomy 6:4-9. We must teach God's Word diligently to our sons and daughters. When we fail to faithfully disciple the next generation, we will experience the same depravity and slide into humanism.

7. Write a brief summary of the book of Judges. What spiritual truths can we glean?

WEEK 1 » DAY FOUR » JUDGES 1

Judges 1 is an overview of what happened after the death of Joshua. It gives us the facts. Chapter 2 goes into a little more detail and gives us Heaven's estimation of their behavior. It is very clear that the Israelites have disobeyed God. They have made covenants with the people of the land and have not broken down their altars (2:1-2).

Read Judges 1.

1. Who does God say was to go up first against the Canaanites?

2. Does Judah completely obey? (Look at verses 3 and 19.)

Tim Keller gives us insight,

> Common, but faithless, sense, begins to prevail here. Judah doesn't trust God; and so they don't secure their inheritance so that they can worship God without compromise. The remaining Canaanites will prove to be a thorn in their side for centuries to come…It is not our lack of strength that prevents us from enjoying God's blessings, or from worshiping God wholeheartedly; it is our lack of faith in *His* strength.[6]

3. Have you ever responded to God's Word by asking someone else to go with you or only half-way obeyed?

4. Where else have you seen this take place in Scripture?

5. Read Joshua 24:14-21. What is Joshua's charge to the people?

6. How do the people respond?

Have you ever responded as they did? Yes, Lord! I will obey! It is often easy to make commitments to the Lord without real follow through. We can become so content to hear God's Word preached or taught and even be moved by what we hear only to leave the church service or Bible study and promptly forget what the Spirit was saying to us.

7. What are some ways you can be more intentional about following through with true obedience?

As we have read through Judges, we have seen how God answers the cries of His people, even when He knows their hearts have not really changed. They just want relief! Yet, He relentlessly responds and moves on their behalf.

Keller makes the application,

> God wants lordship over every area of our lives, not just some. God wanted Israel to take the entire land of Canaan, but instead they only cleared out some areas and they learned to live with idols in their midst. In other words, they neither wholly rejected God nor wholly accepted Him. This halfway discipleship and compromise is depicted by the book of Judges as an impossible, unstable compound. God wants all of our lives, not just part."[7]

8. Read Joshua 1:8. What does God say will ensure success?

Commit Joshua 1:8 to memory and meditate on how you can make this verse a reality in your life.

WEEK 1 » DAY FIVE » JUDGES 2

Judges 2:6-3:6 has been described as a second introduction to the book of Judges. In reality, it is a summary of the entire book. In Judges 2:1-5, we see some remorse and repentance on behalf of the people. We feel somewhat hopeful. But when we look at Judges 3:5-6, we see the compromise that led to their decline: "But they settled among the Canaanites, Hethites, Amorites, Perizzites, Hivites, and Jebusites. The Israelites took their daughters as wives for themselves, gave their own daughters to their sons, and worshiped their gods."

> *It is always impossible to lay blame neatly when one generation fails to pass its faith on to the next one. Did the first generation fail to reach out, or did the second generation just harden their hearts? The answer is usually both. Mistakes made by a Christian generation are often magnified in the next, nominal one. Commitment is replaced by complacency and then by compromise.[8]*
> ~Tim Keller

1. Read Judges 2:1-5. Write the angel of the Lord's message in your own words.

2. Read Judges 2:6-10. How did the Israelites fail to train the next generation and how is this a word of warning for us?

> *All that generation also were gathered to their fathers; and there arose another generation after them who did not know the LORD, nor yet the work which He had done for Israel.*
> Judges 2:10

3. Read Deuteronomy 6:4-9, 20-25. What specific instructions were given to pass on their faith to the next generation?

Knowing what God commands for passing our faith to the next generation, we can readily see the areas we do not measure up or have not obeyed. Consequently, we are seeing many who have been raised around the things of God turn from Him when they leave home and are on their own.

4. What steps can we take to begin to reverse this trend?

5. Are you currently involved in a discipleship group where you are passing your faith and the commands of Christ to the next generation?

A friend sent me a quote recently by Dallas Willard from his book, *Living in Christ's Presence,* "There is nothing wrong with the church that discipleship will not cure. Nothing."[9] If you would like to get involved in discipleship at Bellevue, please contact our Discipleship Ministry or the Bellevue Women office. If you are not a member at Bellevue and your church does not have an active discipleship ministry, ask an older or more spiritually mature woman if you can meet with her and discuss the Bible and the life lessons she has learned and applied.

Many women who have not been formally discipled may feel inadequate. After praying about who you should approach, simply ask if they would be willing to read through the Bible with you and pray with you. The Bible really teaches itself. The accountability of meeting with another person or a small group enables us to follow through on our commitment to read the Bible from Genesis to Revelation. There are many One Year Bibles as well as other formats for reading through the Bible. The key is to choose one that works for you and get started.

We cannot obey what we don't know. God desires for us to be in relationship with Him through His Son, Jesus Christ. It is as you get to know Him through His Word that your heart is changed and your mind is renewed. This is not a passive assignment from God. This is a war against our flesh and the enemy. You can expect resistance, but know this – God has given us everything we need for life and godliness (2 Peter 1:3). It is not in our own strength but in the power of His Spirit!

6. Read Judges 2:11-23. Notate the verses that correspond beside each segment in the sin cycle.

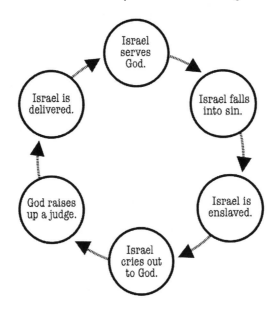

7. How would you describe this sin cycle in your own life?

8. How would you describe this sin cycle in our culture?

God is faithful to the covenant He has made with us. It is our unfaithfulness that leads to dysfunction and depravity. It seems so straightforward and simple. It is simple, but it is not easy. We have a battle against our flesh, the world, and our enemy. The good news is that in Christ we have everything we need for victory. We must appropriate and live out God's Truth and then we will be able to stand firm against the schemes of the enemy, wholly suited up in the armor of God, wielding our sword through prayer.

We will move into the era of the first judge next week. Pay special attention to the way the judges and the people grow weaker as we work our way through this study. Ask the Lord to show you **His** ways that you may know Him.

TIMELY TRUTH

We must appropriate and live out God's Truth and then we will be able to stand firm against the schemes of the enemy, wholly suited up in the armor of God, wielding our sword through prayer.

WEEK 2

When You Live with Idols
Judges 3

Idolatry may not involve explicit denials of God's existence or character. It may well come in the form of an over-attachment to something that is in itself perfectly good...An idol can be a physical object, a property, a person, an activity, a role, an institution, a hope, an image, an idea, a pleasure, a hero, anything that can substitute for God.[1]
~ Os Guinness

Many theologians refer to Judges as the saddest book in the Bible. It chronicles "the story of a nation that had once known the wonderful works of God, a nation with a glorious history, but a nation that turned from its grand heritage to reap a grim harvest."[2] Indeed, Judges is a catastrophic sequel to the book of Joshua. In Joshua, the people were obedient to God and wholeheartedly followed Joshua in conquering the land. In Judges, the next generation is disobedient to God, idolatrous, and often oppressed by their enemies. Certainly, we would be in utter despair reading this tragic account of Israel's history were it not for God's enduring faithfulness which shines brightly against the dark backdrop of His people's recurring idolatry and compromise. David Beldman notes,

> Israel is a culturally and historically rooted example—albeit largely an example of what not to do—of God's people living in God's world under God's rule. Yet, Judges offers readers in the 21st century a picture of God's intentions for his people and a warning about the devastating consequences when God's people fail to live up to their calling—consequences that affect not only God's people but also the unbelieving culture around us and creation as a whole.[3]

Israel's disobedience makes her God's enemy. Strong language, but none the less true! James 4:4 says, "You adulteresses, do you not know that friendship with the world is hostility toward God? Therefore whoever wishes to be a friend of the world makes himself an enemy of God." As we continue our study in Judges, we must remember our own propensity to sin or else we will be in danger of reducing our study to a history lesson about the children of Israel and fail to make appropriate applications to our own habitual sin patterns. May His dealing with Israel serve as both an encouragement and a caution to us.

WEEK 2 » DAY ONE » JUDGES 3:1-4

Read Judges 3:1-4.

1. Why does God allow some of Israel's enemies to remain unconquered in the land? (vv. 1-4)

God did not drive out all the Canaanites from the Promised Land. Instead, He used them to teach and test Israel. Would they obey the commandments of the Lord, which He had commanded their fathers through Moses? As we have already seen in Judges 1-2, sadly, they do not. The children of Israel settle down in the midst of their adversaries, adopting an attitude of peace-at-all-costs towards the enemies of God, including tolerance of their pagan gods.

Tim Keller writes about the belief system that has infiltrated the Israelites:

> It was this belief system which had led to Israel's failure to take all of Canaan; it was this belief system which the ongoing co-existence of the Canaanites encouraged and facilitated. The Promised Land was meant to be a place of worship of the Lord alone; it became the land of worship of the Lord plus.
>
> The people's failure to take all of Canaan both resulted from and represented their failure to give God exclusive lordship over their whole lives. It is not hard to see how this might happen today, as we believers live in a pagan world that offers us a vast array of alternative "gods." The greatest danger, because it is such a subtle temptation which enables us to continue as church members and feel that nothing is wrong, is not that we become atheists, but that we ask God to co-exist with idols in our heart.[4]

How does this happen to a nation that has experienced God's blessing and deliverance? First, the Israelites tolerate the pagan lifestyles of their nemesis, then they accept their heinous practices, and ultimately they adopt their idolatrous ways. Rather than changing their prevailing culture, they become homogenized by it, foolishly attempting to combine the worship of the Lord with idols.

Warren Wiersbe writes:

> God had put a wall between Israel and her neighbors, not because Israel was better than any other nation, but because she was different. Instead of worshipping idols, the Jews worshiped the one true God who made the heavens and the earth.[5]

2. Make a list of the nations that are left in the land. (v. 3)

The geographical spread of these nations bears witness that the evil activity within Israel was not relegated to one section of the community, but demonstrated a national epidemic of idolatry.

T. L. Brensinger notes:

> By testing his community, however, the Lord in fact reveals something significant about Himself. For a test to be genuine, both success and failure must be possible outcomes. Every teacher who knows the joy of evaluating outstanding achievement also knows the pain and frustration of witnessing failure. To give a test, then, implies taking a risk. From all indications, God stands willing to do just that, preferring to use freedom rather than excessive restraint. Whether with Adam and Eve (Genesis 2:16-17), Job (Job 7:17-18), or Jesus Himself (Matthew 4:1-11), God allows testing that can result in failure. As a parent increasingly grants freedom to a growing child, so God's acts of nurturing make room for difficult situations and varying human responses. While this approach at times seems arduous and even unfair, only the possibility of failure provides honest insight and the opportunity for true obedience to shine.[6]

TIMELY TRUTH

Satan tempts us; God tests us. God tests His people in order to reveal the condition of our hearts.

Beloved, learn this about our God. He does not tempt His people to sin. James 1:13 says, "Let no one say when he is tempted, 'I am being tempted by God'; for God cannot be tempted by evil, and He Himself does not tempt anyone." Satan tempts us; God tests us. God tests His people in order to reveal the condition of our hearts. Obviously, God already knows the state of our spiritual lives. The test reveals our maturity (or lack thereof) to us. We must be confronted with the reality of our progressive sanctification in order to make midcourse corrections and to fortify our faith. Without such tests of faith, we would surely come to the erroneous conclusion that we are more spiritual than we truly are!

3. Read James 1:2-4. What is God's purpose for testing our faith?

Don't let it escape your notice—God uses both our successes and our failures. The children of Israel are responsible for the disobedience that led to their dire consequences, but God uses their failures to draw them to repentance and to serve as a cautionary tale for further generations.

God not only uses the enemies of Israel to test the Israelites, but also to teach the art of war to the younger generation who have not yet had battle experience. Judges 2:10 describes the current population of Israel saying, "There arose another generation after them who did not know the Lord, nor yet the work which He had done for Israel." They do not know the Lord or His works on behalf of Israel, including the exodus and the wars of conquest. As a result, the exploits of the previous generation have become secondhand stories to those in need of firsthand experience. T.L. Brensinger notes:

> Israel under Joshua and the elders was faithful, outwardly at last, and living in the fear of God. But a second generation came in—people who had not seen the works of the Lord, who had got the truths from the elders secondhand. They had not come right down to them from God, but they had learned them in an indirect way, and I might add, in an intellectual way, rather than in their hearts. How easy it is for the second generation of any movement to have truth in the head, but not in the heart.[7]

This generation of Israelites has "not experienced any of the wars of Canaan" (Judges 3:1). Therefore, the Lord leaves nations in the land "in order that the generations of the sons of Israel might be taught war, those who had not experienced it formerly" (Judges 3:2). This reference to battle readiness is not just how to fight, but how to fight successfully, depending on the Lord for the victory.

Remember, the current generation has been born after the death of Joshua. Therefore, they have not been part of Joshua's military campaigns in Canaan. Joshua and the armies of Israel did not overcome these nations by their own might or military expertise. God had been their defense. God's help was only granted to Joshua and the whole nation of Israel on the condition of strict adherence to the law of God. The Lord said to Joshua, "Be strong and courageous, for you shall give this people possession of the land which I swore to their fathers to give them. Only be strong and very courageous; be careful to do according to all the law which Moses My servant commanded you; do not turn from it to the right or to the left, so that you may have success wherever you go" (Joshua 1:6-7). The favor of the Lord rested upon Joshua and the Israelites as long as they walked in obedience to the Lord. This new generation needs to learn to rely on the Lord for victory. And although they will fail and fail miserably, God will remain their Faithful King.

Read 2 Timothy 2:11-13.

This is a hallelujah passage concerning the faithfulness of God! Many Bible commentators believe Paul is quoting a familiar hymn in this passage. These verses contain four declarations, each beginning with the word "if."

4. Fill in the following blanks.

   a. If we died with Him, we _____.
      Speaks of salvation and sanctification

   b. If we endure, we _____.
      Evidence of genuine conversion and promise of eternity with Jesus

   c. If we deny Him, He _____.
      Evidence of a lack of genuine conversion

   d. If we are faithless, He _____.
      This is the definition of God's grace!

Even when we are faithless, He remains faithful!! Hallelujah! Tim Keller writes, God relentlessly offers His grace to people who do not deserve it, or seek it, or even appreciate it after they have been saved by it.[8]

We will continue to see Israel's shameful habitual sin patterns as she repeatedly plays the harlot, acting in unbelief and disobedience as revealed through her idolatry. Thankfully, written boldly across the book of Judges is the recurring theme of God's faithfulness. In light of Israel's faithlessness, we should be both astounded and thrilled amidst the daily spiritual struggles and defeats in which we are engaged.

WEEK 2 » DAY TWO » JUDGES 3:5-8

As we saw yesterday, God left the Canaanites in the land to test and teach His chosen people. God said, "Watch yourself that you make no covenant with the inhabitants of the land into which you are going, or it will become a snare in your midst" (Exodus 34:12). By allowing the Canaanites to remain in their tribal allocation, they violate God's direct command to them. Sadly, Israel gradually adopts the lifestyle and the idolatrous worship of their surrounding pagan neighbors, contrary to God's express prohibition.

By engaging in idol worship, Israel transgresses the law. Exodus 20:4-5 says, "You shall not make for yourself an idol, or any likeness of what is in heaven above or on the earth beneath or in the water under the earth. You shall not worship them or serve them; for I, the Lord your God, am a jealous God." Israel's waywardness releases God from His commitment to drive out the Canaanites before Israel. He will no longer remove the nations left in the land when Joshua died. Rather, they will serve a further end in God's program as tools in the hand of God to test the hearts of His people.

Read Judges 3:5-8.

1. What people groups are living among the Israelites? (v.5)

2. List the sins that Israel commits. (vv.5-7)

The initial step into disobedience that sends Israel into their next cycle of sin is their decision to intermarry with those outside the covenant promises of God. "They took their daughters for themselves as wives, and gave their own daughters to their sons, and served their gods" (Judges 3:6). These idolaters gradually turned the hearts of their mates away from God.

3. Read Deuteronomy 7:1-6. What instruction had God given to them through Moses concerning intermarriage?

Contrary to God's law, the Jews intermarry with the nations. Through the act of marriage, the Israelites bring pagans into the most intimate pairing of human relationship. They graft their enemies into part and parcel of their nation and gradually adopt their gods, their religious beliefs, and their worship. Israel lapses into a period of apostasy and the consequences were disastrous. Failure to obey God always is.

Judges 3:7 sadly records, "The sons of Israel did what was evil in the sight of the Lord, and forgot the Lord their God and served the Baals and the Asheroth." The children of Israel sink into idolatry, the antithesis of their national identity as God's chosen people.

4. What does God do as a result of Israel's sins? (v. 8)

5. How many years are the Israelites enslaved? (v. 8)

Since the children of Israel were acting like pagans, God began to treat them as such! Psalm 18:25-26 says, "With the kind You show Yourself kind; with the blameless You show Yourself blameless; with the pure You show Yourself pure, and with the crooked You show yourself astute." Had Israel been faithful to the Lord, He would have sold their enemies into their hands, but they were not. Therefore, God sells them into slavery.

Charles Spurgeon once said "that God never allows His people to sin successfully. Their sin will either destroy them or it will invite the chastening hand of God."[9] One of the lessons Judges shouts at us is that "righteousness exalts a nation, but sin is a disgrace to any people" (Proverbs 14:34 NIV).

6. Read Hebrews 12:5-8. How does the Lord deal with His disobedient child?

God has great compassion on His people and exhibits unprecedented patience. However, without the evidence of repentance followed by a change of direction, His wayward child will come under the discipline of the Lord and reap the consequence of the sin.

7. Write the verses that correspond with the first three segments of the next sin cycle we see in Judges. You will complete this cycle tomorrow as we are introduced to Israel's first judge.

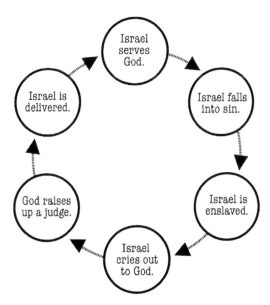

The sin cycle of the children of Israel is seen today whenever God's people turn away from His Word do what is right in their own eyes. God is a good Father, but He will not tolerate sin in the lives of His people.

Paul writes, "Now these things happened to them as an example, and they were written for our instruction, upon whom the ends of the ages have come" (1 Corinthians 10:11). May we humbly continue our study in the Book of Judges, knowing we are equally capable of habitual patterns of sin, and glean the spiritual significance of this dark time in Israel's history with its over-arching theme of the faithfulness of our God and Father.

WEEK 2 » DAY THREE » JUDGES 3:9-11

Today we will finally meet the first of Israel's judges. As you recall from yesterday's study, Israel has forgotten her God. That is, they are no longer controlled by what they knew to be true of Him. They have forgotten to remember what they already know. In Joshua's farewell address, he cautioned the children of Israel, saying, "So take diligent heed to yourselves to love the Lord your God. For if you ever go back and cling to the rest of these nations, these which remain among you, and intermarry with them, so that you associate with them and they with you, know with certainty that the Lord your God will not continue to drive these nations out from before you; but they will be a snare and a trap to you, and a whip on your sides and thorns in your eyes, until you perish from off this good land which the Lord your God has given to you" (Joshua 23:11-13). The children of Israel have been duly warned, yet they do not obey. No wonder they have incurred the anger of God!

Read Judges 3:9-11.

1. Write the verses beside each of the remaining segments of the sin cycle that we began yesterday.

The children of Israel cry out to the Lord. The Lord responds and sends them a deliverer. This scenario reminds us of their experience as slaves in Egypt. "And the sons of Israel sighed because of the bondage, and they cried out; and their cry for help because of their bondage rose up to God. So God heard their groaning; and God remembered His covenant with Abraham, Isaac, and Jacob. God saw the sons of Israel, and God took notice of them" (Exodus 2:23-25).

2. Who does God send to deliver Israel?

This is not the first time we have met Othniel.

3. Read Judges 1:10-15 and make notes on what we already know about Othniel.

Bible scholars do not agree on the exact blood relationship between Othniel and Caleb. It is possible Othniel is the son of Caleb's younger brother, Kenaz, making Othniel Caleb's nephew. Caleb's father's name was Jephunneh (see Joshua 14:6) while Othniel's father's name was Kenaz. Perhaps Jephunnech had died and Caleb's mother remarried Kenaz and bore Othniel, making him Caleb's half-brother. The Hebrew and English translations are ambivalent on this point. Thankfully, we don't have to unravel Caleb's family tree in order to glean truth from this text. By blood and by marriage Othniel belongs to a godly line, a family noted for its courageous faith.

4. What is the key to Othniel's success as a leader? (Judges 3:10)

Othniel, a seasoned warrior, knows the secret to victory–dependence on the Lord. Beloved, this is the essence of spiritual warfare. Paul instructs, "Put on the full armor of God, so that you will be able to stand firm against the schemes of the devil" (Ephesians 6:11). The battle is the Lord's. By faith, we appropriate His power and stand "strong…in the strength of His might" (Ephesians 6:10). The empowering Spirit of God was the secret to Othniel's strength, even as He must be the source of ours as well.

5. Fill in the information on Othniel on the chart on page 11.

The 40-year season of rest and renewal under Othniel ends on a sad note, "Othniel the son of Kenaz died" (Judges 3:11). Unfortunately, Israel does not survive the death of her spiritual leader. Similar cycles of revival throughout church history have been short-lived as well. Why? Because for total healing and permanent peace, we need a leader who does not die.

This story of Israel's first judge Othniel, godly though he was, reminds us of the problem with every human leader and points us to Jesus, our Prince of Peace! Jesus said, "I am the first and the last, and the living One; and I was dead, and behold, I am alive forevermore, and I have the keys of death and of Hades" (Revelation 1: 17-18). Revelation 11:15 says, "The kingdom of the world has become the kingdom of our Lord and His Christ; and He will reign forever and ever." Hallelujah! We serve the righteous Judge who rules and reigns forever!

The cycle of sin remains a recurring problem for all people of faith. Like the Israelites, we can quickly "forget" who our God is and what He has done for us.

6. What spiritual disciplines are required of us to remain mindful of the truth of God's Word in this present age? Put a star by the disciplines that you need to improve and jot down some steps of action that will help you achieve your goals.

Though we dwell in dark days, in a culture, which by and large, rejects our Biblical worldview, we serve a risen Savior, a FAITHFUL KING!

WEEK 2 » DAY FOUR » JUDGES 3:12-30

Israel's next sin cycle begins with the refrain-like statement, "Now the sons of Israel again did evil in the sight of the Lord."

Read Judges 3:12-30.

1. As you read the colorful story of Ehud, Israel's second judge, note the verses that correspond with each segment of the next sin cycle.

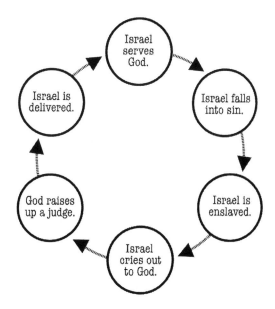

2. How does God respond to Israel's rebellion? (vv. 12-14)

3. Who oppresses Israel at this point in her history? (vv. 12-14)

Week 2 | 47

The Moabites, Ammonites, and Amalekites are not only neighbors; they are relatives. Lot, Abraham's nephew, was the father of Moab and Ammon through an incestuous relationship with his daughters (see Genesis 19:36-38). Esau, the brother of Jacob, was the grandfather of Amalek (see Genesis 36:9-12). They were the first enemies the children of Israel encountered after the exodus from Egypt (see Exodus 17:8-16). The fact that Israel is facing attacks from their kinsmen according to the flesh makes this chapter in their history even more bitter.

How could Israel be so unfaithful to the God who rescued her from Pharaoh, redeemed her by the blood of the Passover lamb, and restored her to the Promised Land? God has systems in place to proclaim His Word and exalt His Name. What has happened? And why are we seeing the same unraveling of the faith even to the point of apostasy in our next generation? God had ordained the priests and the Levites to officiate at the Tabernacle and to teach the law to the people. They were the guardians of the faith, speaking to God on behalf of the people and speaking to the people on behalf of God. The Lord also had instituted the family unit (see Genesis 1:27-28; 2:24). As we saw last week when we looked at Deuteronomy 6, God's design for the family was (and is) to serve as the primary means for passing down the living faith from one generation to the next.

Israel has had forty years of blessings and rest in the land from their enemies. The Israelites had so much to be grateful for and a very recent memory of God's goodness with which to instill in the hearts and minds of their children. And yet, it appears the older generation has failed to instruct the next generation in the ways of God. Dire consequences ensue.

Eglon, the king of Moab, defeats Israel and then sets up headquarters in the city of the palm trees, Jericho. You will recall that Jericho is the place where God gave his people their first major victory when they entered the Promised Land. In a stroke of divine irony, the scene of God's miraculous victory became the stronghold of their enemy.

Before we move on in today's study, we need to address this tragic scenario—the place of victory became a place of defeat. It has been said, "An unguarded strength is a double weakness."[10] We tend to keep our guard up in areas of our weakness, recognizing our vulnerability, and being cognizant of the enemy's schemes to tempt us to stumble. But what about our strengths? We are confident we have successfully fortified these areas. Paul cautioned, "Therefore let him who thinks he stands take heed that he does not fall" (1 Corinthians 10:12). Beloved, identify your Jericho, the place of great victory, as well as your known weaknesses, and carefully guard it against the onslaught of the enemy. May we say with the psalmist, "The Lord has been my stronghold, and my God the rock of my refuge" (Psalm 94:22).

When the children of Israel cry out to the Lord, He raises up a "deliverer for them."

4. What interesting detail do we learn about Ehud? (v. 15)

The original language implies Ehud's right hand is useless, perhaps from a birth defect or a catastrophic injury. In a culture where such infirmity is looked upon with great disdain, Ehud seems to be an unlikely candidate to deliver Israel. Only God!

Ehud is tasked to take the tribute to Eglon, king of the Moabites. Eglon is described as "a very fat man" (Judges 3:17). Culturally, obesity indicated prosperity and was generally looked on favorably.

5. How does Ehud defeat Eglon? (vv. 15-25)

After Ehud kills Eglon and escapes, he blows the trumpet and gathers the armies of Israel. His first step of obedience prepares him for a greater leadership role in the victory against Israel's enemies. Ehud rallies the sons of Israel to battle. "They struck down at that time about ten thousand Moabites" (Judges 3:29). We can assume Moab's defeat signaled for their allies, the Ammonites and Amalekites, to withdraw from the field of battle. "So Moab was subdued that day under the hand of Israel. And the land was undisturbed for eighty years" (Judges 3:30).

6. Fill in the information on Ehud on the chart on page 11.

7. Ehud is an unlikely deliverer, yet God chooses to use him. Read 1 Corinthians 1:26-31. Who does God call to serve His Kingdom?

8. Why does Paul say God chooses unlikely people to accomplish His kingdom work?

9. Is there something God is calling you to do that you are shrinking back from? What is it? Why are you hesitating?

10. What steps of action can you take to respond in obedience?

Ehud teaches us much about how the Lord works in the lives of His people. God uses broken damaged people, who are often on the margins of society, in order to set His power on full display." 'Not by might nor by power, but by My Spirit,' says the Lord of hosts" (Zechariah 4:6). Dark Times. Broken People. Faithful King!

WEEK 2 » DAY FIVE » JUDGES 3:31

The next judge God raises up is a man named Shamgar. Everything we know about this judge is contained in one verse, but it gives us some vital information about this courageous man.

Shamgar lives during a time when the Philistines are beginning to wield their power against Israel. As the decades go on, the Philistines will become a major force against Israel, but at this time they are already posing a threat.

1. What is Shamgar's weapon of choice? (v. 31)

An oxgoad was a strong pole about eight feet long. At one end was a sharp metal point used to prod oxen; at the other end, a spade was crafted to clean the dirt off the plow. Warren Wiersbe observes,

> When God goes to war, He usually chooses the most unlikely soldiers, hands them the most unusual weapons, and accomplishes through them the most unpredictable results.[11]

Shamgar uses the closest facsimile to a weapon he could find because the enemy had already confiscated all their weapons (see Judges 5:8). To go to battle with a farmer's implement rather than military implements indicates this deliverer, Shamgar, was a brave and courageous man of faith.

Interestingly, Shamgar comes from a family that has been infiltrated by the pagans who live around them. Gary Inrig notes,

> Shamgar was not a Hebrew name. It was Canaanite. His father's name, Anath, is the name of the Canannite god of sex and war…his family had completely capitulated to the paganism all around them. They certainly did not prepare Shamgar to be a judge and deliverer of God's people.[12]

His family did not prepare him to lead Israel, but God did.

Since there is no mention of peace being restored to Israel, Shamgar's victory may have been an isolated one, but his contribution was significant enough to warrant mention in the Scriptures. Although the exact reason for the Philistine's oppression is not given, we can assume that Israel once again "forsook the Lord and served Baal and the Ashteroth" (Judges 2:13).

2. Fill in the information on Shamgar on the chart on page 11.

Idol worship by God's people. The concept seems incomprehensible to us and renders us quick to judge the children of Israel, which only further proves that we are blinded to our own propensity to sin. John ends his first short epistle with these words, "Little children, guard yourselves from idols" (1 John 5:21). Obviously, his admonition indicates the early church struggled with idol worship and by implication, idolatry remains an issue for us today.

Historically, most, if not all, Old Testament idols were created carved images. Perhaps the most noteworthy idol was the golden calf the children of Israel fashioned while Moses was on Mt. Sinai receiving the Ten Commandments and instructions for the tabernacle.

3. Read Exodus 32:1-5. What did the people ask of Aaron and what was their rationale for needing it?

4. After fashioning the idol, what did Aaron say about the creation of his hands?

This is one of many examples of idol worship recorded in the Bible. Identifying tangible idols, while loathsome to the Lord, is much easier than recognizing the ones we are prone to worship. These lurk in the hearts and minds of believers, stealing the time and attention that should be reserved for God alone. Idols such as illicit sex, money, success, and power, just to name a few, are prevalent in our culture.

5. Read Colossians 3:1-10. Paul identifies some of the idols of the early church that continue to be a blight on our Christian culture. What are they?

6. The secret to overcoming idolatry is contained in Colossians 3:1-3. Write out Colossians 3:1-3. Underline the portion of Scripture that will keep you from setting up idols in your hearts and minds. Memorize this passage and tuck it in your heart to keep your focus on the Lord.

TIMELY TRUTH

Turning from idols entails two actions— repentance and fixing your eyes on Jesus.

Turning from idols entails two actions–repentance and fixing your eyes on Jesus. Set your mind on Jesus because your life is hidden in Him. As this truth becomes a reality in your Christian experience, you will discover the joy of the Lord overtaking the unholy seduction of an idol.

Jesus must become more beautiful to your imagination, more attractive to your heart, than your idol. That is what will replace your counterfeit gods. If you uproot the idol and fail to "plant" the love of Christ in its place, the idol will grow back.[13]

In order to maintain victory in this area, you must engage in spiritual disciplines such as prayer, reading God's Word, meditating on, and memorizing Scripture, and corporate worship and Bible study. As John MacArthur teaches,

> The way to stand guard against this danger is to be constantly renewing our minds with the truth. It is vital to spend time daily reading God's Word and talking with Him in prayer. Joining with other Christians on a regular basis for worship and teaching (through involvement in a local church) is also essential. The Holy Spirit is our guard against pagan influences of the world, but we are called to do our part in obeying the Bible's teachings.[14]

As we have seen this week, God uses people with clean hearts who step out in faith and trust Him. Othniel, Ehud, and Shamgar have different backgrounds, but they share a common strand. They are all bold enough to trust God and confront Israel's enemies. Will you do the same? Will you step out in faith and allow Him to work through you for His glory?

Dark Times. Faith shines brightest in the dark. Broken people. God uses ordinary (and often broken) people to do extraordinary things through His power. Faithful King. Even when we are faithless, He is faithful! May we be encouraged to live well for Jesus in these dark days that His name might be glorified and magnified!

When An Ezer Leads
Judges 4-5

The purpose of life is not to be happy. It is to be useful, to be honorable, to be compassionate, to have it make some difference that you have lived and lived well. [1]
~Ralph Waldo Emerson

As I sit at my computer today, I am allowing my mind's eye to wander to that time in the future when you will open your workbook to begin this week's study. I envision a puzzled look, perhaps you will even scratch your head when you read the title and contemplate the question, "Just what is an *ezer*?" Actually, the Hebrew word, *ezer*, (pronounced azer with a long a), refers to a "who" rather than a "what" and is defined as a helper.

Ezer is used to describe Eve in Genesis 2:18, "Then the Lord God said, 'It is not good for the man to be alone; I will make him a helper suitable for him.'" God had a specific plan for Eve and for the women who would eventually follow her. Yet Eve's assignment was blurred as she succumbed to the temptation of Satan, and the whole trajectory of mankind was forever changed. Eve's calling as a helper was overshadowed by the legacy of her sin, which frequently dominates our thoughts concerning her. But God has not forgotten. His calling for us, like His for Eve, is secure–we are to be helpers.

In her book, *Lost Women of the Bible*, Carolyn Custis James relates:

> God never abandoned his original blueprint. He never threw out his plan for male and female to bear his image, he refused to retire the *ezer*, and he maintained his vision of the Blessed Alliance. God set his jaw with determination when things were at their worst–Paradise was in shambles and a fig-leafed Adam and Eve were standing there making excuses. God's love never stops. His purposes never change. [2]

Week 3 | 55

As we begin our study of the next sin cycle in the saga of Judges, we will meet an *ezer* named Deborah whom God raises up to assist in the deliverance of Israel. Having fallen again into the trap of idolatry, the Israelites are an unworthy lot, but God has Deborah right in the middle of his rescue strategy. It's an exciting narrative, so let's get started.

WEEK 3 » DAY ONE » JUDGES 4:1-6

Before we get into the heart of the story, let's spend a little more time considering God's design for an *ezer* or helper. Carolyn Custis James provides us a timely reminder: "If we want to recover Eve's true legacy, we must begin where the Bible does–with her creation. We must retrace our steps to the Garden of Eden to retrieve the truth God reveals about Eve before the serpent showed up." [3] God's design for the significant mission of women is revealed in these passages.

1. Consider these verses and record what you learn concerning God's assignment for women.

   Genesis 1:27

   Genesis 2:18

2. What responsibility does God designate for Adam and Eve to perform jointly? See Genesis 1:28.

Carolyn Custis James expounds on God's model to accomplish His purpose: "God was forging a powerful union between the man and the woman that was essential for the challenges they faced together. Eve brought to this alliance everything God called her to be as an image bearer and *ezer*. God's plan to reveal his image through humanity involved both male and female. No where does God's image shine more brightly than when men and women join in serving him together." [4]

While the word *ezer* is frequently used in the context of the marriage relationship, this is not always the case. It can also encompass relationships in which men and women work together to accomplish a purpose, as we will see in the narrative of Deborah. Interestingly, the same Hebrew word is used sixteen times in the Old Testament to describe Yahweh when He comes to Israel's defense in times of trouble.

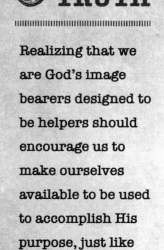

TIMELY TRUTH

Realizing that we are God's image bearers designed to be helpers should encourage us to make ourselves available to be used to accomplish His purpose, just like those women who came before us.

3. Review these verses using the Hebrew word *ezer*, and note what you discover about God as our helper and how this encourages you.

    Deuteronomy 33:29

    Psalm 54:4

    Psalm 118:7

    Psalm 121:1-2

Realizing that we are God's image bearers, designed to be helpers, should encourage us to make ourselves available to be used to accomplish His purpose, just like those women who came before us. "*Ezers* are alive and well throughout biblical history. They come alongside the men in their lives—husband, father, brothers, friends, and colleagues—joining hands to reflect God's image and build his kingdom." [5] One such woman was Deborah—now on to her story.

4. Read Judges 4. On the chart, list the key players in this narrative and document the important facts concerning each.

Name	Pertinent Information

Week 3 | 58

5. Based on Judges 4:1-6, how would you describe the situation in the land of Israel?

Obviously, Israel was in a dilemma. Theologian Gary Inrig describes it succinctly:

> Militarily, Israel was confronted by two awesome facts. First, Jabin had 900 iron chariots, as well as a large infantry. Nine hundred chariots do not sound impressive in a world spending 400 billion dollars annually on armaments, but they represented the very latest in military armaments then. The chariots made it impossible for Israel to defend the valleys and plains. Their military position was nothing less than appalling. Israel was outmanned, outgunned, and out-positioned. They not only lacked iron chariots, they lacked virtually all iron weapons. [6]

6. Have you ever found yourself in a seemingly impossible situation; if so, what was your initial response?

7. Did God show up as your helper and what was the outcome?

With Israel ostensibly challenged beyond her capabilities, one would predict absolute defeat unless you factor in God with His faithful helper, Deborah, into the equation. We will investigate the details more fully tomorrow. No doubt God shows up.

WEEK 3 » DAY TWO » JUDGES 4:4-14

Our study of the Deborah account concluded with a cliffhanger yesterday. Having fallen back into the cycle of sin, the Israelites have been under the iron fist of Jabin for twenty years. In their despair, they cry out to God for deliverance. Through His prophetess, Deborah, God directs them to go into battle against Sisera, the commander of Jabin's armies. The odds are seemingly impossible–destruction appears inevitable.

I can't help but wonder how this scenario has happened again in the life of the Israelites. You would think that they would have come to the realization that the idolatry and sexual perversion so prevalent in the Canaanite culture did not work for them! Yet, here they are again having turned their backs on the God who led them out of Egypt and brought them into the Promised Land. God had established an everlasting covenant with them, and all He has asked for in return is their faithfulness.

1. How do you see the sin cycle of Israel demonstrated in Deborah's story? Note the verses that correlate to each section of the sin cycle on the diagram below.

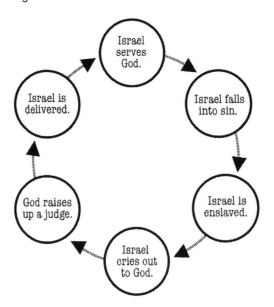

2. What warnings to the Israelites do you observe in these passages concerning idol worship?

   Deuteronomy 4:15-19

   Deuteronomy 31:15-18

3. Read these passages to compare and contrast the Lord God of Israel and idols.

   Isaiah 40:18-26

   Isaiah 44:6-19

While on a mission trip to Kolkata (Calcutta), India, a few years ago, we arrived only to discover that our trip coincided with a festival for the Hindu goddess Kali, the goddess of time, death, and doomsday. She is also associated with violence and sexuality, yet is deemed symbolic of motherly love. As we traversed the city, we noted many street-corner shrines to the goddess where people had left offerings of flowers and food. Later in the week, we visited Dakshineswar Kali Temple, where we were guided through the temple by a Brahmin, a Hindu priest, who explained the history and culture concerning the temple. He noted that we would be able to view the goddess and encouraged us to buy some flowers to place in tribute. We refused to purchase any flowers much to the Brahmin's dismay. Why should we? We serve the living, mighty, Creator God, not a lifeless goddess created by man. "I am the Lord; that is my name! I will not give my glory to anyone else, nor share my praise with carved idols" (Isaiah 42:8, NLT). And neither would we give praise to anyone else. Amen and amen.

Now back to our story.

4. Read Judges 4:4-7. In what two ways is Deborah serving the Lord God, and what do her responsibilities look like?

Surely God called Deborah into significant areas of service that were typically reserved for men. As a prophetess, she relayed the very words of God. She was an *ezer* in the truest sense. Timothy Keller in his book, *Judges for You*, relates:

> Deborah is very different from all the other judges, before and after her. She led from wisdom and character, rather than sheer might. Where Othniel "went to war" (3:10) and Ehud made his assassination plan (3:16), Deborah counseled and guided the people. So she comes closest to being a godly leader of the people, instead of simply a general. She was a judge who led beyond the battlefield. [7]

In Old Testament Israel, there were three great "offices:" prophet, priest, leader (king/judge). Some women (such as Deborah) were prophets; some were judges/queens (Deborah again!). None were priests (Numbers 3:10 and Leviticus 21 show that all priests were men, descended from Aaron). The Old Testament tells us that women are equal in value, dignity and ability, created as they are in God's image and given dominion under him over his creation (Genesis 1:26-28). It also shows us that women were free to use their gifts in any role but that of priest. God shows his Old Testament people that men and women are equal, but not equivalent.[8]

5. What does the Lord command, through Deborah, for Barak to undertake, and what promise does He make? (vv.6-7)

6. Record Barak's response and how you interpret his answer. (v.8)

Timothy Keller suggests two different interpretations of Barak's comment. "The more pessimistic view sees Barak asking Deborah to go with him, and refusing to go if she doesn't, as a timid lack of faith."[9] In the second alternative, he submits, "His desire to take Deborah with him is not disobedience, but done out of a recognition that Deborah is a godly woman who speaks God's words. Why wouldn't he want her with him?"[10]

7. How is Barak described in Hebrews 11:32-34, and does your opinion of his response to Deborah change as a result?

Examine Judges 4:9-14 to grasp the context for the next part of our study.

Deborah agrees to go with Barak, and the two head fearlessly toward Mount Tabor, making a stop to pick up ten thousand men from Zebulun and Naphtali at Kedesh. Then, they rush on in faith to carry out their assignment from God.

8. Take a few moments to pinpoint these key locations pertinent to the storyline on the map on page 7 in your workbook. Record any observations you make regarding them.

   Mount Tabor

   Kedesh

   Kirshon River

As we conclude our study today, the Scripture reminds us of Barak's valor. "So Barak went down from Mount Tabor with ten thousand men following him" (Judges 4:14b). Never mind the nine hundred iron chariots. Never mind Sisera's fully equipped army. Never mind Israel's lack of spears and shields. Barak was marching down Mount Tabor with Deborah's words still ringing in his ears, "Arise! For this is the day in which the Lord has given Sisera into your hands; behold, the Lord has gone out before you" (Judges 4:14).

Barak's forces were no match for Sisera's; but Sisera's were no match for God![11]

My friend, what will be your response when God asks you to do the outwardly impossible? Will you march down that mountain, or even up the mountain, leading other valiant women behind you? Remember, God will go before you.

WEEK 3 » DAY THREE » JUDGES 4:15-24

At the end of our study yesterday, Barak is charging down Mount Tabor with ten thousand men following him. Though the situation looks hopeless, they are trusting in the God of Israel and what He has instructed them to do through the prophetess, Deborah. Their hope is in God. Let's pick up where we left off.

Read Judges 4:15-16.

1. What happens during the battle? You might want to turn to Judges 5:4, 20-21 for some additional insight.

2. In verse 15, the word "routed" is used to describe what God did to Sisera's army. Look up the Hebrew word *hamam* in your Hebrew dictionary or at Biblestudytools.com (under Old Testament Hebrew Lexicon); and record what you learn.

I was interested in what I discovered about *hamam* in the Lexical Aids in the Hebrew-Greek Key Word Study Bible: "to agitate. To put in motion, impel, drive, put to flight, disperse; to agitate, trouble, confound; to utterly destroy, make extinct. Used to denote the confusion God created among the enemies of Israel."[12] This description denotes God working in a powerful way in the situation. It was not happenstance—indeed not—God was acting on behalf of His people.

3. The Old Testament records many instances when God intervened in the affairs of Israel. Read these two accounts and note what you discover.

   Exodus 14:21-28

   2 Kings 6:15-18

God bears no resemblance to the lifeless idols of the Canaanite people. He is a miracle working God. And He comes to the defense of His people when they call on Him. As twenty-first century Christians, however, we tend to think that perhaps the age of miracles is over.

4. Do you believe that God performs miracles on behalf of His people today?

As you contemplate this question, I would like to share with you some excerpts from an article entitled "Miracles of the Six-Day War" by D. Thomas Lancaster:

> On May 15, 1967, as the people of Israel celebrated Independence Day (Yom Atzmaut), the Israeli government received some bad news. It had been exactly nineteen years since the declaration of the Jewish state and the beginning of the War for Independence. That same day in 1967, it seemed that the unfinished war had resumed as the Israeli government learned of Egyptian forces massing in the Sinai under the command of Gamal Abdel Nasser. Egypt, Syria, and Jordan, along with Iraq, went on alert and placed their forces on a war footing, ready for invasion and war against Israel.
>
> Israel declared the closing of the straits to be an act of war, but the nation cowered at the thought of facing the combined forces of Egypt, Jordan, Syria, and Iraq. The allied Arab forces could boast nearly half a million troops, almost twice what Israel could muster, even with its reserves. Backed by the Soviet Union, the Arabs possessed more than twice the number of tanks and four times the number of aircraft Israel had.
>
> The Israelis solemnly prepared for a massive slaughter. They readied hospitals and designated whole national parks as cemeteries for the anticipated casualties. A spirit of fear and despair hung over the nation. It seemed that the dream of a Jewish state, so recently realized, was about to be snuffed out. People spoke pessimistically of a looming second Holocaust, but a few rabbis and holy men predicted a miraculous salvation.
>
> By June 5, the outbreak of hostilities seemed inevitable. Five Egyptian divisions of ground troops and two divisions of armor occupied the Sinai, ready to roll into Israel. Hundreds of tanks stood ready opposite Eilat, prepared to topple the Negev. The Jordanian army had placed thousands of soldiers and hundreds of tanks in the West Bank and along Israel's eastern border. Reinforcement from Iraq stood ready. On the northern border, Syrian soldiers on the Golan Heights dug in for a long fight.

Before the Arab nations could strike, Israel launched preemptive airstrikes against Egyptian airfields. As the Israeli Air Force took to the sky, the first miracle of the war occurred. Jordanian radar detected the planes and tried to warn Egypt, but the Egyptians had changed their coding frequencies the previous day and had not yet updated the Jordanians with the new codes. The message never went through, giving Israel the element of surprise. The Egyptians had no time to react. The Israeli Air Force destroyed six Egyptian airfields and hundreds of Egyptian planes. In a single day, Israel destroyed the Egyptian and Syrian Air Forces.

On the first day of the war, the Israeli ground forces had overrun the strategic road junction at Abu-Ageila to gain access to the central route into the Sinai Desert, sending a wave of panic through the Egyptian command. In Bible times, God often assisted the people of Israel on the battlefield by throwing the Canaanites, Philistines, Arameans, and other enemies into panic and confusion. By the second day of the Six-Day War, the Egyptian army had fallen into that same kind of confusion. Orders from Egyptian commanders contradicted good sense, calling for unnecessary retreats and withdrawals.

The Israeli army expected to face a serious battle at the heavily defended Kusseima outpost in the Sinai, but as they drew near, they heard explosions. When they arrived, they discovered that the Egyptians had destroyed their own equipment and abandoned the base. At other bases, the Egyptians had not even bothered to scuttle their equipment before fleeing.

After the Egyptian minister of defense, Field Marshal Abdel Hakim Amer, heard about the defeat at Abu-Ageila, he inexplicably ordered all his units in the Sinai to retreat to the west bank of the Suez Canal. Some members of the Egyptian army offered the Israelis initial resistance, but soon they all fled their positions, leaving their heavy equipment behind. Israeli ground troops advancing into the Sinai found numerous Egyptian positions simply abandoned, with tanks and heavy armor left in perfect condition. They acquired so much abandoned Egyptian armor that after the war they had enough to outfit five new brigades. [13]

5. After reading this account of the early days of the Six-Day War, what is your response?

God routed the Arab coalition during the Six-Day War just as He had done with Sisera's army. Though outnumbered, Israel claimed a quick and decisive victory and doubled their territory. Thousands of Jews wept and offered prayers of thanksgiving at the Western Wall. God had interceded on behalf of His people.

As we pick up our storyline, we note that Sisera's army is dead, and Sisera alone escapes. His nine hundred chariots, which outwardly had appeared to be his greatest strength, had become his chief liability when God entered the equation. He flees on foot looking for a safe place to hide.

Read Judges 4:17-24.

6. Who is Heber the Kenite, and how does he fit into the storyline? Take note of Judges 4:11-12 as well.

7. Why do you think Sisera feels safe in the tent of Jael, and what is the outcome of his visit?

As a woman in a nomadic tribe whose job it was to set up the tent, Jael would certainly have known how to use the implements she used to kill Sisera. Some have criticized Jael for her lies and the murder of Sisera, and indeed God instructs us to do neither. Dale Ralph Davis addresses this issue:

> Of course, I could be missing something, but it seems to me that the Bible is pro-Jael. Frankly, that does not bother me at all. Sisera, who "severely oppressed" (4:3) Israel and probably enjoyed raping captive Israelite girls (5:30), was not exactly Mr. Clean. Nor should this narrative bother you. But if it does, put the problem on the back burner for a while, for the story does not intend to raise a moral problem but to rehearse Yahweh's salvation. [14]

8. Who is the hero in crushing Jabin?

Timothy Keller reminds us: "It was the Lord who spoke to, and through, Deborah; the Lord who went ahead of Barak and then gave him victory; and the Lord who handed Sisera over to Jael....God is the Rescuer, acting according to His will, not his people's merits; so He deserves the glory." [15] Absolutely–to God be the glory!

WEEK 3 » DAY FOUR » JUDGES 4-5

What a marvelous account of God's divine intervention and deliverance on behalf of His people is found in Judges 4. During our study, we met Deborah, Barak, and Jael–individuals whom God used to accomplish His purpose in overturning the domination of Jabin and Sisera over Israel. There is no indication that they were extraordinary people, but they were called people, called to serve and lead. You might consider the concept of serving and leading an oxymoron, but nothing is further from the truth. Jesus, the God-man, the leader and King of the universe, spoke about His purpose when He said, "just as the Son of Man did not come to be served, but to serve, and to give His life a ransom for many" (Matthew 20:28). To emulate Jesus–serve!

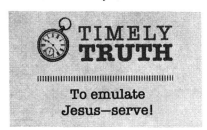

TIMELY TRUTH

To emulate Jesus—serve!

Today we will concentrate on what good leadership looks like. Actually, much may be discerned through an observation of Deborah and Barak from the narrative in Judges 4. So, take a few moments to review the passage before you get started.

1. Evaluate the actions of Deborah and Barak and record the leadership strengths which they displayed as they responded to the crisis before them.

Deborah	**Barak**

2. How were their strengths beneficial in the situation they faced?

Deborah served in a dual capacity as judge and prophetess during this difficult time in Israel's history. While we do not know how long she had served previously, we understand that she possessed great influence as she heard cases, rendered judgments, and spoke the very oracles of God. Obviously, God had called her and placed her in this position of leadership.

Jaye Martin, in her book entitled *Women Leading Women*, reflects on a key component to godly leadership: "When I think of leaders in the Bible, several come to mind. Nehemiah, Moses, Deborah, Joseph, Daniel, Paul, and Lydia are just a few. These were great men and women who chose to follow God. They became great leaders because God had gifted them but also because they allowed God to lead them." [16]

In a society where so many are espousing their ideas and their agendas, it is uplifting to be reminded just Who is in charge. Jaye Martin continues:

> God is the original, ultimate leader. Good leadership principles come from Him and from who He is. They flow out of His character. When God's leadership principles are followed, people will find success in carrying out His plan in His way. Ultimately, God is in control. He is the source of truth and the foundation for everything. He is the true foundation for leadership. He is the original leader.

> The definition of leadership is built on the foundation of the Creator Leader, God Himself. To be an effective leader, one must base her leadership on God. This is a servant style of leadership that balances the characteristics of who He is with what God created that person to be. When we understand who He is, we will then understand the characteristics that are essential for us as leaders. [17]

Once we solve the issue of Who is in charge, next comes the key element in our service. Jaye observes:

> Follow-ship becomes the great challenge. We need leaders who will follow the Leader. We need leaders who, on a daily basis will look to Him before they look to make a name for themselves. Whether leadership is given or learned is not the key issue; the key issue is that to be effective leaders, we are to be obedient on a moment-by-moment basis to the leading of the Holy Spirit. [18]

3. Do you consider yourself a leader? Why or why not?

4. How does Deborah refer to herself in Judges 5:7, and what significance do you derive from the title she gives herself?

I believe that Deborah was presenting herself as a spiritual mother to Israel—one who listened to God and shared what He said. On Mother's Day, I discovered an article by Bible teacher and author Jen Wilkin entitled "Mothers in the Church." Here are some excerpts of her insightful thoughts:

> Every believing woman who grows to maturity becomes, in her time, a spiritual mother to those following behind, whether she ever becomes a mom in physical terms. She fulfills that most basic calling of motherhood: nurturing the helpless and weak to maturity and strength. She helps the young believer to nurse on the pure milk of the Word, faithfully teaching basic doctrine and modeling the fruit of the Spirit. She sacrificially makes herself available, like the mother of a newborn infant, allowing her schedule and personal needs to be inconvenienced for the sake of caring for the spiritually young and vulnerable. And she understands the work to be not a trial but a sacred duty, finding deep delight in the wobbly first steps of faithfulness and stuttered first words of truth.
>
> Not only may spiritual infants fail to recognize spiritual mamas, but spiritual mamas may fail to recognize themselves as such. We may underestimate the need or question our ability to meet it. Or we may hesitate to extend ourselves out of a fear of commitment. But a motherless church is as tragic as a motherless home. Guiding the spiritually young to maturity is not solely the job of the vocational pastor, the elder, or the Sunday school teacher. The church needs mothers to care for the family of God. We must rise to our responsibility, eagerly searching for whom the Lord would have us nurture. [19]

5. What are you currently doing to lead or mentor someone else?

6. Last week you were asked if you were shrinking back from something God is calling you to do. If your answer was "yes", are you making progress with your action steps of obedience?

As a college student, I responded positively to God's call on my life, and after graduation, I left for a two-year assignment with the North American Mission Board of the Southern Baptist Convention. When my assignment was concluded, I did not feel led to go to seminary, so I moved to Memphis to teach school in the inner-city. I joined Bellevue Baptist Church where I met my husband. While we were very actively involved in the life of the church, I would wonder from time to time whether I had misread what I believed was God's call on my life. As I ruminate on it, I now realize that it was in accordance with God's timing. Indeed, God did have a task for me, but it didn't exist at the time. In the meantime, God wanted to develop within me some skills and spiritual maturity that I would need.

Preparation for ministry begins long before the opportunity arises. A well-known speaker and author once shared with me that God had called her to study every day while her children were at school—every day from nine until three. Not long after our conversation, she was able to publish her first Bible study. And she was ready because she had been faithful to study God's Word.

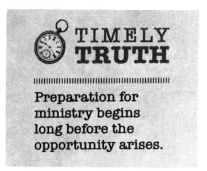

TIMELY TRUTH

Preparation for ministry begins long before the opportunity arises.

As a movement began among women to seriously study the Bible, I discovered my passion for working with women and watching their lives change through experiencing God and His Word. That fledgling idea became a full-blown movement known as Women's Ministry. When Bellevue began a Women's Ministry, I became a volunteer and the rest is history. God equipped me through my volunteer service in the church and other organizations to do what He had in mind all along. Thus, God opened the door for me to serve in Women's Ministry as the director at Bellevue Baptist Church for over twenty-four years. God's call is sure, and His timing is perfect. What a blessing!

7. What do you consider as the most important characteristic of a Christian leader?

As I reflect on my years of ministry, I would say that the all-important characteristic for service would be an intimacy with God and a knowledge and love for His Word. Other skills can be learned from the countless books on leadership. But knowing God is experiential. It cannot be absorbed by merely reading a book. It is a relationship and is a crucial element if you are to serve God. Don't let the enemy convince you that you have no gifts to offer, and there is nothing for you to do. God has an infinite number of opportunities for His *ezers*. How will the world know if we don't share what we have ascertained from the Word, for that is where all the answers to life's issues are?

Now a word from Beth Moore: "Your God is with YOU. He's the one who has called you, gifted you and sent you into your sphere of influence to do good works He planned for you before creation. He thought you were a fine choice. Quit trying to be somebody you're not. You, filled with His Spirit, are quite enough." [20]

The Lord is looking for a few good *ezers*. Will you, like Deborah, answer His call?

Now the God of peace, who brought up from the dead the great Shepherd of the sheep through the blood of the eternal covenant, even Jesus our Lord, equip you in every good thing to do His will, working in us that which is pleasing in His sight, through Jesus Christ, to whom be glory forever and ever. Amen.
Hebrews 13:20-21

WEEK 3 » DAY FIVE » JUDGES 5:1-31

As we approach the conclusion of our study in Judges 4-5, we have come to a delightful divergence from the narrative that we studied in chapter 4. A new genre emerges as we explore chapter 5–poetry. This ancient poem takes the form of a song of praise to Yahweh for His deliverance. Written by Deborah, the memorial hymn would serve to remind Israel, both the present generation along with generations to come, of God's covenant faithfulness to them. These songs, of which there are several examples in the Old Testament, including The Song of Moses (Exodus 15) and many psalms of David (for example, Psalm 18), were frequently used in public worship as an encouragement to praise the Lord.

Read Judges 5:1-5.

1. When do Deborah and Barak sing this song of praise to God, and what significance do you attach to their timing?

Deborah calls kings and rulers and all of Israel to praise the Lord and reminds them of His commitment to Israel at Sinai, where the Lord Himself met with the people and proclaimed His covenant with them. Deborah desires to communicate that the same Yahweh had fought their battle for them and won the victory.

2. Review Exodus 19:16-19 and describe the scene when God met with Israel at Sinai.

3. What does Deborah describe in verses 4-5, and what additional information do you gain from verses 20-22?

4. How does this turn of events change the course of the battle?

The Women's Evangelical Commentary spotlights an interesting tidbit regarding the storm:

> Particularly in the northern region where Jabin king of Canaan was defeated, the Canaanites revered Baal as a storm god who rode the clouds and brought the rain. The song flaunts Baal's impotence by describing what happened when the Lord marched to war.
>
> The Israelites had feared the Canaanites' nine hundred chariots, but the thundering sounds of Barak's ten thousand-man army flowing down Mount Tabor, under Yahweh's direction and accompanied by a storm, may have struck fear in the hearts of the Canaanites. Verses 19-21 also speak of "the waters of Megiddo" and "the river Kishon" as sweeping away "the kings of Canaan," as well as heaven's stars fighting against Israel's enemies, suggesting that the Lord brought against the seemingly invincible chariots a dreadful storm that filled the riverbed and mired the Canaanites' war machinery. [21]

God's miraculous intervention in the battle leaves Sisera's army decimated and the god of the Canaanites' undermined in the eyes of his worshippers—for what man-made idol can withstand the God of the universe? God hijacks what appeared to be a decisive victory and turns a dry riverbed into a raging morass. Baal is no match for Yahweh. Absolutely not.

Now Deborah recollects what life was like before God's deliverance and calls on all Israelites, great and small, to sing!

5. Scan Judges 5:6-8. Describe life in Israel under the domination of Jabin and Sisera.

6. Why has war come to the gates of Israel?

When the Israelites harden their hearts and turn their backs on Yahweh to embrace the Canaanite idols, consequences ensue, and war materializes at their gates. He will not share worship. He holds mankind accountable. The prophet Isaiah reminds us: "But those who trust in idols, who say, 'You are our gods,' will be turned away in shame" (Isaiah 42:17, NLT).

Deborah directs our attention next to the roll call of the tribes in verses 13-18 where she enumerates the tribes who volunteered for the battle and those who, for some reason, failed to assist. Also, you will note that two tribes, Judah and Simeon, are not listed, probably due to their location in the southern-most district of Israel.

7. Record the six tribes that volunteered for the battle and the four who did not participate along with their excuses. As you research the answer to the question, turn to the map on page 7 and note the location of each tribe.

Gary Inrig communicates some perceptive information:

> There is one thing we should notice about these four and one-half tribes who did not respond to God's call. None ever again made a significant contribution to the cause of God. Asher virtually vanished except for a brief involvement with Gideon. Dan nosedived into apostasy; the two and one-half tribes on the east of the Jordan were overrun repeatedly. The chief victims of the reluctant spirit were the possessors of that spirit. They lived for themselves, refusing to risk what they had, and, as a result, they lost what they had. [22]

Warren Wiersbe likens their response to the church today when he comments: "The people of God today are not unlike the people of Israel when it comes to God's call for service: some immediately volunteer and follow the Lord; some risk their lives; some give the call serious consideration but say no; and others keep to themselves as though the call had never been given."[23] Perhaps we should pause and evaluate our decision-making process. What is our first response? Is it "yes" even though the request sounds frightening or beyond our capabilities? Or do we count the cost based on what it will cost us—in time, money, energy? We must not ignore God's call; He values obedience.

8. Contrast how Deborah portrays Jael and the mother of Sisera and record your perceptions (verses 24-30).

Deborah concludes her triumphant song with a two-fold prayer reminiscent of the blessings and curses found in Deuteronomy. "Thus let all Your enemies perish, O Lord; But let those who love Him be like the rising of the sun in its might" (Judges 5:31).

As I studied this victory song written by Deborah, I began to ponder the times in my life when the Lord delivered me. There have been countless times, no doubt, but a few of them have been all too obvious, when I could not doubt his intervention on my behalf. Are you musing about your own deliverance by now? I think I want to write my own song—won't you join me? By now, I know you are probably thinking, "I don't write poetry!!!!!" But, Deborah's song is written in free verse—no rhyming, no rules. How can we go wrong?

The writer of Hebrews states, "Through Him then, let us continually offer up a sacrifice of praise to God, that is, the fruit of lips that give thanks to His name" (Hebrews 13:15). Let's offer Him praise from a grateful heart. Use the space below to write your own song of praise.

MY SACRIFICE OF PRAISE

When You Triumph Over Fear
Judges 6

God doesn't call the brave. He makes brave those He calls. [1]
~J.D. Greear

As we meet the next man God will use to deliver His people, we meet someone who is not a valiant warrior or a man of undeniable strength and confidence. Rather, Gideon is fearful, hesitant, and insecure. I cannot speak for you, but I have certainly identified with these feelings at times in my life. Praise be to God, He does not leave us in our state of weakness! Here's a spoiler alert: this weak and fearful man is praised in Hebrews 11 as one of the prophets "who through faith conquered kingdoms, administered justice, and gained what was promised…whose weakness was turned to strength; and who became powerful in battle and routed foreign armies" (Hebrews 11:33-34, NIV).

Dear sister, do not fall prey to the enemy who assaults you with lies of insignificance, failure, or lack of ability to serve God in mighty ways. Gideon may not have started heroically, but he triumphs over his fear and experiences the mighty hand of God on his life.

WEEK 4 » DAY ONE » JUDGES 6:1-6

We closed last week with a victorious song of praise and celebration. As a result of conquering Sisera, Deborah and Barak sing a proclamation of God's goodness and faithfulness (Judges 5). It is fair to say that Deborah is respected as a wise leader, one who wants to serve God and give Him all glory and honor. She has great insight and confidence and is an outstanding woman in Old Testament history.

1. Let's quickly review the closing of Judges 5. What are the Israelites experiencing in verse 31?

All seems to be going well for the Israelites and "there was peace in the land for forty years" (Judges 5:31b, NLT). Sadly, we will see how quickly that changes. But before we begin to criticize those stubborn Israelites, let us consider our own lives and the sin cycle we have observed throughout this study. Reflect back on a season of prosperity, abundant blessing, peace and calm. In the midst of bliss, have you found yourself shrugging your shoulders at the Lord? The enemy goes back to his age-old tactic of causing us to doubt. He deceives us into believing we don't **really** need God right now. We thrive with "peace in the land" for weeks, months, or even years, and but then lose our fervor and desperation for Him. And that is when we find ourselves falling into sin once again.

The story of Gideon opens with the children of Israel doing evil in the sight of the Lord. As a result of their sin, God delivers them into the hands of the Midianites for seven years. J. Vernon McGee paints this backdrop:

> The Midianites and the Amalekites moved as a disorganized nomadic tribe. They were raiders. They would raid the crops and supplies of others. They generally took their families with them. In fact, they took all that they had with them. They would pitch tents as they moved along. By sheer numbers, they overwhelmed the inhabitants of the land. The children of Israel fled from their homes and lived in caves and dens.[2]

As we closed out the account of Deborah and Barak last week, we came to the stage of the sin cycle where Israel is serving God again and experiencing peace (top circle of the diagram). Judges 6 immediately opens with the next phase of the cycle.

2. Read Judges 6:1-6. Record the verses that best correspond with each segment on the diagram. (Hint: This passage only covers 4 of the segments. You can also turn to *The Judges of Israel* chart and fill in the second and third column for Gideon.)

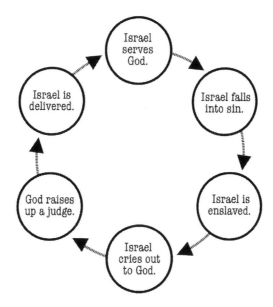

3. Describe the cruelty of the Midianites toward the Israelites (vv. 2-5).

4. What instruction does Moses give the Israelites in Deuteronomy 28:1-2, 15?

5. What consequence for disobedience does Moses give in Deuteronomy 28:43?

In Judges 6, The Israelites have finally hit rock bottom.

6. What has happened to them (Judges 6:6a)?

Week 4 | 79

7. How do the Israelites respond in the last part of verse 6?

Finally, after seven years, they turn to God and cry out to Him. They can no longer take the oppression from the Midianites. Once again, God has become their last resort.

8. What does Proverbs 3:11-12 tell us about the Lord's discipline?

9. What does this tell us about His heart for the Israelites and His heart for us?

Discipline can be painful, but it can also be a gift of grace from our Heavenly Father.

One theologian observes,

> "He loves you too much to let you keep living the way you are. He longs to be at the center of your life. So He has designs in our troubles, and they are always for our good." C.S. Lewis said it like this, 'God whispers to us in our pleasures, speaks in our conscience, but shouts in our pains. It's His megaphone to rouse a deaf world.'"[3]

He is a good, good Father. His faithfulness is unfathomable. Sometimes the lesson comes with great pain, but it always comes with greater love and a desire to restore.

TIMELY TRUTH

A desperate cry rouses the ear of our Heavenly Father.

Tomorrow, we will see God coming to rescue His people once again as He provides an answer for their cry. We, like the Israelites, are often slow to respond to the Lord's discipline or call, yet He is never slow in responding to our cry for help.

A desperate cry rouses the ear of our Heavenly Father. He will lean in closely, listen and respond when He brings Gideon to the stage.

WEEK 4 » DAY TWO » JUDGES 6:7-23

Before we move along through Judges 6, let us spend some time observing the Israelites cry to the Lord and, more interestingly, how He graciously responds.

Tim Keller explains, "So far, though more oppressive, the cycle is following its normal route. Now we expect God to raise up a deliverer, a judge (as in 3:9, 15; 4:4, 6-7). But instead, 'when the Israelites cried to the LORD because of Midian, He sent them a prophet' (6:7-8). God's first response to the people's cry is *not* to send a savior or salvation, but to give them a sermon! The prophet comes and helps them to understand why they are in the trouble they are in. He wants them to understand where their idolatry – their sin – has led them."[4]

We must pay close attention to the response of the Israelites here. God sends a prophet to speak to the hearts of His people. The nature of the "sermon" suggests that their cry is one of regret rather than repentance. Keller says, "God sends the prophet to convict of sin *before* He sends the judge to rescue from oppression."[5]

1. What does 2 Corinthians 7:10 teach us about sorrow over sin?

2. How have you personally experienced the difference between godly sorrow and worldly sorrow (repentance versus regret)?

God desires to move us from regret to repentance. As we see in this account, God answers the cry...even though it is not one of brokenness or a sincere desire to turn from sin. Keller describes it this way, "The heart has not become disgusted with the sin itself, so the sin remains rooted."[6]

Before we move forward, take a few moments to evaluate your own heart. Is there sin that you only regret? Or is your heart grieved because you have grieved the heart of God?

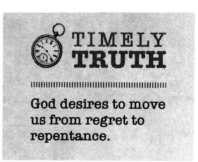

TIMELY TRUTH

God desires to move us from regret to repentance.

3. Are there sin patterns that are deeply rooted in your life for which you have not truly repented? Do you worry more about the consequences of your sin or damaging your relationship with God? Journal your responses to these questions.

4. What does God's response in Judges 6:7-8a display about His character?

5. Write out Romans 5:8 to be reminded of a beautiful truth about the heart of God.

These passages of Scripture display God's holiness and mercy. He offered grace to us even **before** we repented by sending Jesus Christ to save us **while** we were still sinners. Keller says, "God will never compromise on His holiness, nor on His grace. The way to hold together, and appreciate, both God's perfect standards and His endless compassion is to grasp more deeply the cross of Christ, where the two meet so gloriously."[7]

We often find ourselves frustrated at God's response to our difficult circumstance. Let's be honest. If the choice is ours, we would prefer instant deliverance over learning a lesson. Would we not? Dale Ralph Davis reminds us,

> Like Israel, we may want escape from our circumstances while God wants us to interpret our circumstances. Sometimes we may need understanding more than relief; sometimes God must give us insight before He dare grant safety. Understanding God's way of holiness is more important than absence of pain. God means to instruct us, not pacify us.[8]

6. Can you recall a time when you experienced the kindness of God in this way? Consider sharing with your small group how God's delayed deliverance imparted wisdom to you.

Read Judges 6:7-10. Let us close out today's study by taking "sermon notes" from the prophet's message to the Israelites.

7. What reminder of the past does God give through the prophet? (vv. 8-9)

8. What statement does God make about Himself? (v. 10)

9. What admonishment or instruction does He give the people? (v. 10)

A recurring theme throughout the Old Testament is one of remembrance. God calls His people to remember the great things He has done. What an important and powerful tool in the life of a believer! We must make a habit of recalling the wonderful things God has done and continues to do for us. This is paramount in battling the lies of the enemy and this sin-sick world.

Close out today by reviewing God's call on the life of His children. This is true in Judges 6:7-10 and it also is for New Testament believers, including us.

10. Read Ephesians 4:1. Record the call on your life as a follower of Jesus Christ.

The motive for Christian living is not that we might gain something we don't have but that we might live up to what we already have in Christ. [9]
~Warren Wiersbe

WEEK 4 » DAY THREE » JUDGES 6:11-24

What the world may view as trash, God sees as treasure. In the words of my pastor, Steve Gaines, "God must love ordinary people. He sure made a lot of us."[10] As Paul writes in I Corinthians 1:27 (NLT), "God chose things the world considers foolish in order to shame those who think they are wise. And he chose things that are powerless to shame those who are powerful."

In yesterday's study, we saw an unnamed prophet sent by the Lord in response to the cry of the Israelites (Judges 6:7). Today, we will meet Gideon. The Lord sends a special messenger (many believe a pre-incarnate Christ) to deliver an important message to Gideon. As I Corinthians 1:27 tells us, God often chooses the weak and insignificant to do a mighty work and accomplish His perfect will. Gideon is no exception.

Read Judges 6:11-24. (This passage will allow you to fill in the tribe for Gideon on *The Judges of Israel* chart.)

As our text opens today, we see Gideon hiding out. He is threshing wheat at the bottom of a winepress. In case you are unfamiliar with these farming tasks, let's take a crash course in "Wheat Threshing and Winepress 101."

> Threshing was the process of separating the grains of wheat from the useless outer shell called chaff. This was normally done in a large area, often on a hill, where the wind could blow away the lighter chaff when the farmer tossed the beaten wheat into the air. If Gideon had done this, however, he would have been an easy target for the bands of raiders who were overrunning the land. Therefore, he was forced to thresh his wheat in a winepress, a pit that was probably hidden from view and that would not be suspected as a place to find a farmer's crops.[11]

Let's face it. Gideon is a coward. He is not portrayed as a brave and courageous warrior ready to march head on into battle. He is hiding out with the hopes of avoiding the backlash of the abhorrent Midianites.

How quickly, though, the Lord turns the tide. Verse 11 speaks to Gideon's cowardice. Verse 12 speaks to Gideon's future.

1. How does the angel of the Lord refer to Gideon in verse 12? (Read several translations.)

I want to pause here and share a personal experience. The Lord has graciously allowed me the privilege of being part of the writing team for several Bible studies. For those that do not know, our writing team is comprised of five women from our church. I am the youngest and most inexperienced of the bunch (by far on the experience level!). I sit in meetings with these dear women who are my most treasured mentors and heroes of the faith. They have invested h in various ways. I will be eternally grateful; they will be eternally

f once again surrounded by intellectual minds and experienced writers. ...ting my mind with thoughts of inadequacy and unworthiness. I listened ...with my assignment. As I sat down a few days later and began digging into the account of Gideon, my mouth dropped open. I sent the following to one of my writing partners and dear friends.

> In all honesty, my flesh struggles with this whole writing thing. I am bombarded continuously with thoughts of, "What in the world can I offer?" As I sit around the table with you ladies and look around at the immense wisdom of you all, the experience, the vision, etc., I am often intimidated. I fought back tears yesterday as we talked (and I mostly listened) and just sat in awe that God would allow little ole me to be a part of this…such incredible kingdom work.
>
> So I sat down this morning with the intention of penning an outline for my first week. I didn't expect that I would really begin writing…but God had a different plan. I laid my heart out before Him and I just began writing. My mind was absolutely flooded with truth and revelation.
>
> And then I saw the parallel for me and Gideon. I would have never pictured myself to be anything like him, but I saw it. Timid, afraid, small in his own eyes, insignificant, hiding…all of it. And in verse 12 (early in the story!), God calls him a "mighty hero" in my translation. He called a coward a hero! He immediately filled my heart to overflowing, and I was confident that He would finish this work to which He's called me. It will have nothing to do with me. He doesn't need my skill or expertise. He needs my heart, my open hands, my facedown surrender and a willingness to obey with every ounce of myself.

This is true for Gideon. This is true for me. And for you. Available heart. Open hands. Facedown surrender. Willingness to obey.

In his series on Judges, J.D. Greear says, "When God calls us, He doesn't see us or define us by the condition we are in. He sees us and calls us according to what He's predetermined to make us into in Christ."[12]

2. Is the Lord calling you to something in which you are hesitant to follow? What is holding you back?

Not only does God call Gideon a mighty hero (before he actually was one), but He gives the promise that, "The LORD is with you!" God not only sees what we **will** be, but He also promises to be with us every step of the way. We do not have to fulfill His call apart from His presence.

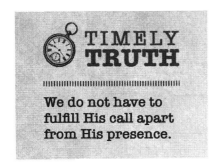

We do not have to fulfill His call apart from His presence.

Gideon's first response to the promise of God's presence is doubt and he "questioned God about the problems he and his nation faced and about God's apparent lack of help."[13] Our human nature is quick to blame God for calamity when our problems often come as a result of disobedience and sin. The adversity the Israelites are facing is a result of their failure to obey Deuteronomy 6:5, which says, "Love the LORD your God with all your heart and with all your soul and with all your strength."

3. Read verses 14-16 and record God's promises to Gideon.

We read in the remaining text (vv. 17-24) that Gideon needs assurance that God will truly help him. He asks to prepare an offering for the Messenger, to which He agrees and patiently waits. We see the graciousness of God again as He ministers to Gideon's doubting heart.

4. What takes place in verses 21-24 and how does Gideon respond?

5. As modern day Christians, we easily cast judgment on Gideon's fear, doubt, and unbelief, but how often we do the same. Read the following verses and record the answer God gives for our unbelief.

   Genesis 18:14

   Job 42:2

   Luke 1:37

   Philippians 4:13

> *'But I will be with you.' Basically, God has nothing else or more to offer you. You can go through a lot with that promise. It does not answer your questions about details. It only provides the essential. Nothing about when or how or where or why. Only the what, or better, the Who. 'But I will be with you.' And that is enough.* [14]
> ~Dale Ralph Davis

'OUR » JUDGES 6:25-32

call on Gideon's life. Our text ended with Gideon building an altar
... is Peace (v. 24).

...e? Gideon has answered the call of the Lord. He was immensely
... el of the Lord face to face and built an altar as an act of worship.
Shouldn't he be prepared to go fight those Midianites?

Read Judges 6:25-32.

Warren Wiersbe says of Gideon, "God assigned him a task right at home to show him that He would see him through. After all, if we don't practice our faith at home, how can we practice it sincerely any place else? Gideon had to take his stand in his own village before he dared to face the enemy on the battlefield."[15]

Gideon belongs to a family of Baal worshippers. If he plans to fight the Midianites in the name of the Lord, he will have to go against his own family, including his father, Joash.

1. What specific instructions does God give Gideon in verses 25-26?

2. Why such a demand? (Reflect on Matthew 6:24 as you give your answer.)

God is preparing to deliver Israel, but He wants them to be prepared for deliverance. This will require a purging of their hearts. Gideon is given specific instructions for destroying his father's altar to Baal and the Asherah pole standing beside it. He is then to sacrifice a bull on this very altar while using the wood of the Asherah pole as fuel for the fire. No corners are to be cut. No stone left unturned. God is bidding Gideon to completely rid this place of anything pointing to idolatrous worship.

In his commentary on Judges, Dale Ralph Davis states, "God cannot safely trust His good gifts to those not fully given to Him."[16]

This causes me to ponder the idea of revival. I am confident that many Christians long and fervently pray for revival in our cities and nation. I know the heartbeat of my own church is to be a catalyst for spiritual awakening. As a Christ-follower and mother of young boys, I long to see darkness penetrated by light. I desire to see a world ceasing to reject the truth of Jesus Christ, and believers experiencing "…far more abundantly beyond all that we ask or think, according to the power that works within us" (Ephesians 3:20b).

So we must ask ourselves, "What am I doing in my own life, in my home, to prepare for revival?"

Just like the Israelites, we belong to a God who delivers. We belong to a God who hears the cries of His people and longs to answer. But are we prepared to receive it? Do we have our own altars to Baal or Asherah poles still standing in our lives? Do we go along with the patterns of our family or societal norms even if they are contrary to the Word of God?

3. Take some time to honestly reflect. Are there altars to other "gods" still erect in your heart?

4. What can you do today to ensure God reigns unchallenged on the throne of your heart?

Tim Keller offers this powerful challenge,

> Before they can throw off the enemies around them (the Midianites), they have to throw off the enemies among them (the false idols of Canaan). This is always the main way that we get renewal in our lives. God will not help us out of our obvious, visible problems until we see the idols that we are worshiping right beside the Lord. They have to be removed first. Gideon is essentially being told here to make God the Lord of every area of life. We are not to use God to get what we really want, but we are to see and make God the One we really want.[17]

Perhaps this sounds contrary to the idea that God uses the available, not the qualified. Do not misunderstand what God is asking of Gideon. Remember where Gideon was in the beginning of the story. He was hiding and afraid, not qualified to lead an army into battle against a fierce enemy. God does not require that we be all cleaned up and perfectly prepared for the call. He does require, though, an undivided heart and an abandoned will.

5. What do the passages below teach you about God's preparation in the small or hidden things?

   1 Samuel 17:32-37

   Matthew 25:21

"It's worth noting that true believers can't build an altar to the Lord unless first they tear down the altars they've built to the false gods they worship. Gideon had privately built his own altar to the Lord (Judges 6:24), but now he had to take his public stand, and he had to do it without compromise. Before he could declare war on Midian, he had to declare war on Baal."[18]

6. What do you need to do privately (with God, in your home, among close family/friends) before God can use you publicly?

The last verses in today's text speak volumes. Not only does Joash come to Gideon's defense before the angry townspeople, but Gideon is also given a new name.

7. How does Joash respond to the angry mob in verse 31?

8. Why do you think he responds in this way?

9. What name is given to Gideon in verse 32?

Gideon learned a valuable lesson on that day. He may have been fearful, but nevertheless, he obeyed God. God protected him by working in his father's heart and raising him up to defend Gideon in the face of those who wanted him dead. Verse 32 tells us that Gideon is called Jerub-baal, which means, "Let Baal defend himself." God received glory and Baal was exposed!

Consequently, Gideon is empowered to march on with boldness and confidence and answer "YES!" to the call God has placed on his life. Israel will be forced to choose "to prop up Baal or worship at the altar of Yahweh."[19]

What about you? You may not be leading a brigade into military conflict, but you are engaged in a war. We have been called to be salt and light to a lost world. God calls us to opportunities for ministry. Many of us are mothers, grandmothers, or mentors. Clean off the shelves of your heart from any clutter that distracts your single-minded focus on Yahweh.

He is worthy. He **alone** is worthy.

WEEK 4 » DAY FIVE » JUDGES 6:35-40

Putting out the fleece. We've all heard this phrase, and I suspect we have varying opinions on this familiar passage of Scripture. I do not claim to have the answer, so I will share what the Lord has taught me in my study (a little taste from both schools of thought) and encourage you to seek the Holy Spirit for revelation. Honestly, He's shown me several truths from this passage while highlighting His attribute of grace and love for me. So let's dig in!
Following the destruction of the altar of Baal and a name change for Gideon, we see in today's text the armies of Midian, Amalek, and the desert tribes of the east forming an alliance against Israel and crossing the Jordan to come into Jezreel. The heat is being turned up against Gideon and the Israelites.

1. It is time for Gideon to act. What happens to Gideon in verse 34?

2. As we seek to do God's will, what encouragement do we receive from Zechariah 4:6?

Warren Wiersbe tells the following story,

> When a group of British pastors was discussing the advisability of inviting evangelist D.L. Moody to their city for a crusade, one man asked, "Why must it be Moody? Does D.L. Moody have a monopoly on the Holy Spirit?" Quietly one of the other pastors replied, "No, but it's evident that the Holy Spirit has a monopoly on D.L. Moody."[20]

3. What characteristics do you see in the lives of those that are empowered by the Holy Spirit? Do you desire to see any of these manifested more in your life?

Gideon was obedient in destroying the altar of Baal and the Asherah pole, bringing reformation to the land. The Spirit of the Lord had come upon him, so when he sounds a horn as a call to arms, many neighboring tribes come to his aid to wage war against the Midianites. Obedience brings blessing, and there is no match for the Spirit of the Lord.

4. What does Gideon do in the remaining text of Judges 6? (vv. 36-40)

Is Gideon's request a lack of faith or a desire to understand God's nature? Is God's answer indicative that Gideon had not sinned in his asking?

Let's look at the idea of unbelief. If we find ourselves demanding a sign or giving God a condition for our obedience, I believe "putting out the fleece" is a dishonorable method for hearing from God and determining His will. However, as we see in the account of Gideon, God graciously honors his request. One commentary said, "Many people have criticized Gideon for this action. If, however, it was so wrong and sinful, why did God respond?"[21]

I don't know that I'm qualified to determine whether or not Gideon sinned, but I do know that we serve a loving and gracious God, even when we fall short in our belief.

5. What does the father of the boy with the unclean spirit pray in Mark 9:24?

6. How does Jesus respond in Mark 9:25?

Jesus grants the father's request even as the father proclaims an element of unbelief. God will do the same for us, just as He did for this father and for Gideon.

7. Have you experienced a circumstance where you have said to the Lord, "I do believe; help me overcome my unbelief!"? What did the Lord teach you?

Another point of view I came across was that of faith building. Tim Keller explains it this way:

> Gideon was very specifically asking God to show him that He was not one of the forces of nature (like the other gods), but was sovereign over the forces of nature. Gideon, then, was not looking for "little signs" to help him make a decision. He was really seeking to understand the nature of God. He was very specifically addressing the places where his faith was weak and uninformed. We cannot use this as a justification to ask for little signs and signals. Gideon was not doing so – he was asking for supernatural revelation from God to show him who He really is. This therefore is not about how to make a decision. This is about how we need to ask God to give us a big picture of who He is. Gideon's request was for help to build up his faith. God, in His grace, responded (twice!). When we make the same request, God graciously responds: by pointing us to the fullest, final revelation of His character and His purposes – the Lord Jesus.[22]

We can take comfort in this account of Gideon. Do you identify with him? The hesitancy. The unbelief. The "I-just-need-to-be-sure" moments. Whether it is a mighty position like Gideon or reaching out to someone who needs the love of Jesus Christ, you have been called. God is calling every child of His to love, serve, share, and minister to someone. Do not fall prey to the enemy's lie that your calling is measly and insignificant.

What if Gideon had stayed holed up in that winepress? What if he hadn't listened to the prophet and answered the call to rise up? What if he hadn't boldly destroyed the altar of Baal at the risk of losing his family? What if he hadn't blown that ram's horn, with the Spirit upon him, and summoned his allies?

TIMELY TRUTH

God can handle your weakness and bouts of unbelief. God wants to reign unchallenged in your heart. He wants your obedience and your YES!

What if we stay hidden in our homes and churches? What if we don't listen to the call to penetrate our city and nation with the truth of the gospel? What if we don't boldly stand against the darkness and the lies of the evil one? What if we don't use the power of the Holy Spirit to join arms with our brothers and sisters for the sake of the Gospel?

We do not have to do it in our own power. Gideon didn't. We do not have to do it alone. Gideon didn't. We do not have to do it perfectly or without fault. Gideon didn't. We do not have to do it apart from human frailty and weakness. Gideon didn't.

God can handle your weakness and bouts of unbelief. God wants to reign unchallenged in your heart. He wants your obedience and your YES!

In the midst of it all, we see a gracious, patient and loving God.

We will find that God will gradually school this man until He brings him to the place where Gideon can see that there is nothing in him. Then God will use him to win a mighty battle. [23]
~J. Vernon McGee

And He will do the same for you.

WEEK 5

When You Win the Battle but Lose the War
Judges 7-8

It is true that the faith, which I am able to exercise, is God's own gift. He alone supports it, and He alone can increase it. Moment by moment, I depend on Him. If I were left to myself, my faith would utterly fail.[1]
~George Mueller

In our study last week, we were introduced to Gideon, a most unlikely hero, living during a dismal period in Israel's history. Long forgotten was the dramatic delivery God had provided the Israelites through Deborah and Barak. Again, they had relapsed into an evil sin cycle as they pursued the idolatrous practices of their Canaanite neighbors. So, the Lord placed them under the crushing oppression of the Midianites, who arrived each harvest like a plague of locusts and ravished their crops, leaving them destitute. When they cried out to the Lord for deliverance, He sent a prophet to rebuke them for their unfaithfulness. Yet the Lord was not finished with them. He had selected Gideon, an extremely improbable candidate, for the next judge to liberate His people. In a theophany, the Lord Himself appeared to Gideon and greeted him as "mighty warrior." Thus, God began to graciously guide the reluctant Gideon into the development of a walk of faith.

Despite Gideon's fears and misgivings and his frequent need for reassurance, the words of God become his faith anchor. Trusting in the God who had accepted his sacrifice, he bravely (well, he might have done it at night) accomplishes the destruction of Baal's altar, raises an army, and awaits his next instructions from the Lord. This week we will hopefully build our faith as we scrutinize Gideon's story and the marvelous works that God executes through Gideon.

Before we begin, let's reflect on our walks of faith. May I ask you a personal question? Whose words do you cling to? Do you listen to the culture–do you listen to a friend–do you listen to your emotions and those voices in your head–or do you listen to God? Gideon had to make that decision and so do we. Erwin Lutzer reminds us, "Christians are a minority in an increasingly hostile culture. We are exiles, not geographically, but morally and spiritually."[2] There are

TIMELY TRUTH

God's inerrant Word will never steer you wrong. Listen to it. Do it.

countless words swirling around us today—many I had never even encountered until recent months. They are vying for our attention and adherence. Remember what Jesus prayed for the disciples before His crucifixion: "I have given them your word and the world has hated them, for they are not of the world any more than I am of the world" (John 17:14, NIV). God's inerrant Word will never steer you wrong. Listen to it. Do it. As they used to say when I was a girl, "Got your ears on?"

WEEK 5 » DAY ONE » JUDGES 7:1-8

Read Judges 7:1-8.

1. What view greets Gideon when he looks out over the Jezreel Valley the next morning? (vv. 6:33, 7:1)

2. Relate the first directive that God shares with Gideon. What was His purpose for it?

The background and explanation for God's guidance for Gideon can be found in Deuteronomy, which served as God's instruction manual for Israel.

3. Review Deuteronomy 20:1-4, 8 and record what you discover about the reasoning behind God's instruction.

Tim Keller comments further on this concept:

> The reason it was good to send them home is a practical one. Fear is contagious, as we can often see in Judges. When any significant body of soldiers panic and flee, it can sap the determination of everyone and lead to a rout. Though it was surely discouraging to lose these numbers, it was still very practical to let them go...for the morale of the army. [3]

Imagine Gideon's surprise and dismay when 22,000 men turn to journey home. The odds seemingly are stacked against them. Can't you just envision Gideon leaning in to hear what the Lord had to say? Would angelic forces come to rescue them? Perhaps a new source of recruits will be revealed. Surely Yahweh will not expect them to fight with only 10,000 soldiers. Then God speaks.

4. What additional instructions does God communicate to Gideon regarding the soldiers, and what does He promise?

Commentators maintain various opinions concerning the appropriate mode of drinking water in this scenario, usually touting one method over another based on the vigilance and alertness of the soldiers. In *The Books of History*, J. E. Smith notes: "Commentators are divided on the question. Many feel that God simply used the drinking exercise as a mechanism for further reducing the force to 'faith size.' Certainly the text is silent about any military superiority of the 'lappers' over the 'kneelers.'"[4] Nevertheless, God chooses 300 men and proclaims that Midian will be delivered into their hands. It will undoubtedly be a walk of faith for Gideon and his extensively pruned army.

5. Divide the number of Gideon's forces into the amount aligned on the side of Midian (Judges 8:10) to determine to what extent the Israelites were outnumbered.

6. How does Gideon respond when God says to send the "kneelers" home? (Judges 7:8)

Presume what must have been going through Gideon's thoughts as he observes his troops when they depart for home. Don't you imagine he is bombarded with assaults from the enemy to doubt God? From a human perspective, it appears to be a disastrous strategy. But Gideon decides to trust God even when the plan seems untenable.

Gary Inrig conveys how God works in the life of a believer: "God does not call us to believe in ourselves and in our own adequacy. Rather, He strips us bare, taking us down to the place where we must depend on Him. Then, in grace, He takes us by the hand and teaches us that we can trust completely in Him."[5]

7. Outline some steps describing how believers can react in faith when faced with an impossible situation.

It has been inspiring to contemplate Gideon's transition to God-confidence, but we might also want to ponder what the Midianites are thinking as the changes take place in Gideon's camp. Warren Wiersbe furnishes us some thought-provoking insight:

> It is clear from 7:14 that the Midianites knew who Gideon was, and no doubt they were watching what he was doing. I've often wondered what the enemy spies thought when they saw the Jewish army seemingly falls apart. Did it make the Midianites overconfident and therefore less careful? Or did their leaders become even more alert, wondering whether Gideon was setting them up for a tricky piece of strategy? [6]

Looks like we have a potential David vs. Goliath kind of conflict brewing—an army boasting 135,000 well-trained and well-equipped soldiers facing Gideon's 300 men. But wait. Israel has a secret weapon—Almighty God.

See you tomorrow, my sisters.

WEEK 5 » DAY TWO » JUDGES 7:9-15

As we concluded our study yesterday, Gideon and his army of 300 men appear to be facing insurmountable odds. When night came, I imagine an uneasy repose fell upon the camp—and perhaps no slumber at all for some. Presumably Gideon is restlessly recounting the details of God's instructions and trying to evaluate the weight of His promises. With our knowledge of God from His Word, we might wonder why he would ever doubt that God would and could do all that He promised. However, we must remember that Gideon lives in a family that advocates Baal worship and in a culture that has been severely oppressed by the Midianites for seven years. In all those years, Yahweh has never come to their rescue. The Israelites have turned their backs on God so why, he might have thought, will He deliver them now? Yet, Gideon has followed through on everything God has commanded thus far, but the odds seem pretty frightening—to be outnumbered 450 to 1.

Examine Judges 7:9-15 to discover what happens when God speaks to Gideon again.

1. When does the Lord speak to Gideon, and what does He say? (v. 9)

2. What accommodation does God make for Gideon based on his fear?

Our gracious God knows our frames and our insecurities just as He was aware of Gideon's. Tim Keller reminds us of this truth: "God goes out of his way to reassure his people."[7] God recognizes that a little reconnaissance trip is exactly what Gideon needs. Keller continues: "What does this incident tell us about our Christian lives? First, that God is the great Reassurer. He is the one who takes initiative here. Gideon needs this visit to the quaking enemy camp in order to get him to worship, trust, and attack—but he does not ask for it."[8]

3. Upon arriving at the Midianite camp, what does Gideon observe in the valley?

No doubt, as Gideon is contemplating the masses before him, both men and animals, his mind returns to the promises God has made to him.

4. Scan Judges 6 and 7:1-15 and record each commitment from God to Gideon.

Take some encouragement from Tim Keller to heart: "When we know we are weak, we need to remember that God is strong. We also need to be reminded of the truth that those things which stand opposed to us are not as strong as they often appear." [9] This truth will become very clear to Gideon as he happens to eavesdrop on a conversation between two Midianite soldiers.

5. Describe the dream that the soldier relates, and what is the other soldier's interpretation?

It is interesting to note that barley bread was made from a common grain that usually was eaten by the poor and animals. After seven years of the Midianite marauders stealing their crops, the Israelites certainly fit into that category. Clearly, the nomadic Midianites could be represented by the tent. And it suddenly becomes clear not only to the soldiers but also to Gideon. God is about to do something utterly amazing. The victory will be theirs.

6. What is Gideon's immediate response?

7. When was the last time that God's graciousness to you resulted in an eruption of spontaneous worship?

As I wrote the last question, my heart was pierced with the thought, "Why would I ever take the goodness of the Almighty God, Creator of the Universe for granted?" Could it be that I have forgotten the wretchedness of my own sins and the majesty and righteousness of God? That alone would make me cower before Him aside from grace. That He would love me enough to provide the ultimate sacrifice of Christ for my salvation is beyond comprehension. Oh, to exalt Him, to bow before Him, to worship.

A few days ago, I read a quote from A. W. Tozer that is both thought provoking and pertinent to the consideration of our worship. Ponder it carefully as you read it:

> The church has surrendered her once lofty concept of God and has substituted for it one so low, so ignoble, as to be utterly unworthy of thinking, worshiping men. This she has not done deliberately, but little by little and without her knowledge; and her very unawareness only makes her situation all the more tragic. The low view of God entertained almost universally among Christians is the cause of a hundred lesser evils everywhere among us. [10]

Gideon totally understands the hopelessness that is Israel aside from God. He comes away from his reconnaissance trip with a renewed faith and an exalted view of God. Scripture is replete with examples of how an accurate view of God generates worship. Is your view of God a precise one, and does it inspire genuine worship? Let's review some passages from the Biblical narrative where God is both exalted and worshiped.

8. Examine these passages drawn from the lives of men from the Old Testament and document what you ascertain about God and worship.

    Exodus 34:5-8 (Moses)

    1 Chronicles 29:10-13, 20 (David)

    2 Chronicles 7:1-3 (Solomon)

    Daniel 2:19-23 (Daniel)

9. Share a favorite passage of Scripture that moves your heart into worship.

Emboldened by God's revelation through the dream, Gideon makes his way back to the camp and shouts, "Get up! The Lord has given the Midianite camp into your hands" (Judges 7:15b, NIV). God had promised, and He always keeps His promises. And off to battle they went—300 men against what appears to be a multitude. Nevertheless, God was on their side.

WEEK 5 » DAY THREE » JUDGES 7:16-25

As we begin our study today, we catch a glimpse of Gideon, a new man infused with God-confidence, addressing his troops. Warren Wiersbe comments about his transformation: "No longer do we hear him asking 'If–why–where?' (6:13) No longer does he seek for a sign. Instead, he confidently gave orders to his men, knowing that the Lord would give them victory." [11] The plan was simple though unorthodox.

Read Judges 7:16-25.

1. Outline Gideon's battle strategy and evaluate how it measures up to traditional warfare.

2. In a critique of Gideon's plan, what would the average battle strategist fail to consider?

A jar, a torch, and a horn are unconventional weapons to say the least. Apparently, there is not a single shield, or arrow, or sword to be found among the equipment. Yet Gideon's faith must have been contagious for the 300 men followed him to the Midianite camp to engage in battle. Gary Inrig pens this timely reminder, "It is not our responsibility to understand how God is going to keep His Word and accomplish His work. It is our responsibility to obey Him and do what He commands." [12]

3. When do Gideon and his men implement their plan, and how do the Midianites respond?

Inrig continues his creative narrative of the nocturnal events:

> Now Gideon put God's plan into action. He waited until the middle watch had just been posted. That was about 10:30 P.M., when some of the men had been asleep for three or four hours and were in the deepest part of their sleep. The men who had just been relieved from guard duty would still be moving through the camp, and the men who had just gone on duty would still be rubbing sleep out of their eyes.
>
> Suddenly, there was a huge noise all around them. The rams' horns were signaling an enemy attack. Then the clay pitchers smashed on the ground, sounding like armies clashing into one another. The Midianites looked up, and they were surrounded on three sides by lights and torches. Finally, a great shout shattered the silence, "A sword for the Lord and for Gideon." To the half-asleep men, everything that moved became the enemy. Every shadow was an Israelite. In all the confusion, the camels stampeded, and in the chaos and tumult that resulted, the panicked Midianites began to slaughter one another. [13]

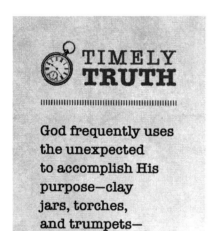

TIMELY TRUTH

God frequently uses the unexpected to accomplish His purpose—clay jars, torches, and trumpets—unexpected but definitely effective.

Just reading that account could certainly raise your heart rate. The Lord indeed has a flair for the dramatic. God frequently uses the unexpected to accomplish His purpose—clay jars, torches, and trumpets—unexpected but definitely effective. Perhaps the Apostle Paul was referring to this event when he wrote, "But we have this treasure in jars of clay to show that this all-surpassing power is from God and not from us" (2 Corinthians 4:7, NIV). No one could deny that it was God's all-surpassing power that achieved the victory.

Another amazing account of how God won a victory for Israel is found in Joshua 6 in the narrative of the battle of Jericho. Let's review this familiar description of God's powerful intervention for His people. Be on the lookout for some more trumpets.

4. Scan Joshua 6:2-20 and compose a brief synopsis of this display of God's power.

What a faith builder. Now back to our story.

5. What are Gideon's soldiers doing in the midst of the mayhem? What are they not doing?

Believing they are undoubtedly outnumbered, the Midianites flee, and Gideon recruites some reinforcements to pursue them.

6. In which direction would you presume the Midianites would flee? (Hint: check Judges 6:3) Locate their potential escape route on the map on page 7.

7. Which Israelite tribes join in the chase? Pinpoint the locations of their territories on the map.

8. What accomplishments are attributed to the tribe of Ephraim? (Judges 7:24-25)

It is noteworthy that when the Midianite princes Oreb (meaning raven) and Zeeb (meaning wolf) are captured and executed, the places of their deaths are named after them. Thus, those sites became known as the rock of Oreb and the winepress of Zeeb and served as memorials to remind the Israelites of God's goodness to them. Interestingly, a winepress and a rock played a significant role in Gideon's story as well—the winepress where Gideon was hiding when the angel of the Lord first appeared to him and the rock where Gideon's sacrifice was consumed revealing the angel as the Lord Himself. The defeat of the Midianites becomes a milestone of God's faithfulness among the Israelites.

God had previously commissioned another memorial as the Israelites crossed the Jordan River to enter the Promised Land. You probably are already familiar with the storyline, but it is found in Joshua 3-4 if you would like to read the entire account. Though the Jordan was at flood stage, the Lord blocked the water upstream as the priests carrying the Ark of the Covenant stood in the center of the river, and all the people crossed on dry ground. Joshua reminded them that the God who could stop the rushing river was with them and would go before them as they proceeded into the land that He had promised Abraham. According to the Lord's instructions, one man from each tribe selected a stone from the riverbed before the waters flowed quickly back into place. Joshua stacked stone upon stone to create a monument. Then He conveyed to the Israelites, "In the future, when your children ask you, 'What do these stones mean?' tell them that the flow of the Jordan was cut off before the ark of the covenant of the Lord. When it crossed the Jordan, the waters of the Jordan were cut off. These stones are to be a memorial to the people of Israel forever" (Joshua 4:6-7, NIV). God had demonstrated His miraculous power among His people, and they must remember.

The year was 1989, and Bellevue Baptist Church was preparing for a move from its cramped mid-town Memphis location to a sprawling campus in Cordova. Reminiscent of the Joshua passage we just considered, the theme for our move was "Claiming our Canaan." For twelve weeks, a young boy dressed in Biblical attire would scale the steps to the platform with a large stone in his arms and ask the question, "What do these stones mean?" In reply, a Bellevue member would recount a memory of when God did a marvelous work in the life of our church. The Saturday before our move, a procession came through the gates at the new church and included were the boys carting their stones as we claimed our Canaan. My younger son was one of those boys who carefully stacked those stones of remembrance creating a fitting memorial. He is now a minister of the gospel shaped by the legacy of this church and the great God–Father, Son, and Holy Spirit–upon whom it is built. God has been so good to us.

A time of reflection seems in order to contemplate the times in your life when God has acted on your behalf. Perhaps it came in the form of guidance in a decision, of healing from a disease, or even in a downright deliverance as in the case of Gideon. I think it is time to make our own memorials using our stones of remembrance.

9. On this timeline, chart your stones of remembrance listing the dates and circumstances. Spend a few moments in prayer to pour out your gratitude to the Lord.

Let's close today with a thought-provoking quote from Tim Keller:

> We can, and should, live our lives and order our memories not only historically but theologically—not simply recollecting what happened, or what we did, but searching out what God was doing. This keeps us from over-honoring ourselves in success, or despairing in our struggles. Part of the key to enjoying peace is to be continually praising the Lord for what He has done, and is doing, for us, because the story we tell of our lives is not so much about us, as about Him. [14]

WEEK 5 » DAY FOUR » JUDGES 8:1-21

As we concluded our study in chapter 7 yesterday, Gideon and his band of 300 were in quick pursuit of what was left of the terrified Midianite army. Gideon's battle strategy and Yahweh's miraculous intervention had routed the Midianites, leaving them in confusion and decimation. The Israelites no doubt watched in awe as the Lord God performed a miracle without them even raising a hand in battle. They had acted in faith, and He had executed the impossible. The principle of this quote by Jack Graham could have been their mantra: "Do what is possible by faith and God will do the impossible. When we come to the end of our might we experience the almighty power of God." [15]

Regrettably, as the narrative of Gideon's life continues in chapter 8, we will notice some changes in him, subtle at first, but then more obvious. Gone is the fearful, hesitant Gideon who trusted in God alone and listened to His instructions. Instead, we will observe a man whose choices will substantiate our premise for the week: that it is possible to win the battle, yet lose the war. I trust that all of us want to finish well. It was certainly on the mind of the Apostle Paul as he wrote to Timothy, "For I am already being poured out as a drink offering, and the time of my departure has come. I have fought the good fight, I have finished the course, I have kept the faith; in the future there is laid up for me the crown of righteousness, which the Lord, the righteous Judge, will award to me on that day; and not only to me, but also to all who have loved His appearing" (2 Timothy 4:6-8).

Read Judges 8:1-21.

Gary Inrig weighs in on this chapter with some thought-provoking observations: "Unfortunately, as we come to Judges 8, we are faced with a story of compromise, defeat, and backsliding–the last chapter in the life of a man who knew the greatest victory of faith set down in the Word of God." [16] God has achieved the victory, but our human nature is so apt to attempt to seize the credit as our own. It is never pretty when pride and ingratitude show up.

> As you read this chapter, you will not find one word of spontaneous praise, gratitude, or thanksgiving to God. Nothing is more indicative of the spiritual condition of Israel than this. Before they ever approached Gideon (to become king), they should have been pouring out their hearts in praise to the God who gave them victory, but that never occurred to them. They did not have the singing faith of Moses or Joshua or Deborah. Their hearts did not ring with praise to their God. [17]

1. Do you see any signs of ingratitude, pride, or other inappropriate attitudes in the criticism from the Ephraimites, and how does Gideon respond to them?

Scripture does not specify exactly the precipitating factors in the Ephraimites' complaint, but we do know they have a few things to boast about. Being the largest and most important tribe, they count Joshua as one of their own. Even the tabernacle is located in their territory. And, they have just hunted down and killed the two Midianite generals, Oreb and Zeeb. Or perhaps, they are disappointed not to be sharing in the significant spoils of battle. Regardless of their motivation, Gideon treats them with graciousness, and the conflict is alleviated. However, Gideon's reaction to the next two groups is distinctly different. So, let's delve into this portion of chapter 8.

2. What request does Gideon make to the officials of Succoth and Peniel, and how do they reply?

3. Can you speculate as to why these two towns refuse to help?

4. Describe Gideon's retort to each and in what way does he follow-up later?

Perhaps Gideon's actions seem unconscionable to you. After all, the inhabitants of these towns are fellow Israelites. Since we see no indication of the Lord's intent in the Scripture, theologians offer differing evaluations of Gideon's deeds. We will look at two views. The New Bible Commentary offers this opinion:

> Gideon's humility and caution completely disappear. He now throws diplomacy to the wind, demanding support with threats of retribution on those who fail to give it. And in marked contrast to the earlier phase of Gideon's career, there is no longer any reference to the Lord being involved in what he does. It is clear that what he now achieves is by his own strength of character and tactical skill, not by reliance upon the Lord. [18]

Now consider what Warren Wiersbe has to say:

> Why didn't Gideon show the people of Succoth and Peniel the same kindness that he showed to the Ephraimites and simply forgive their offenses? For one thing, their offenses were not alike. The pride of Ephraim was nothing compared to the rebellion of Succoth and Peniel. Ephraim was protecting their tribal pride, a sin but not a costly one; but Succoth and Peniel were rebelling against God's chosen leader and assisting the enemy at the same time. Theirs was the sin of hardness of heart toward their brethren and treason against the God of heaven. [19]

The next snapshot we see of Gideon shows him, having tracked and captured the Midianite kings, interrogating them about a previous event.

5. What do you discover about a potential motive for Gideon's relentless pursuit of Zebah and Zalmunna?

6. What does Gideon ask his son, Jether, to do, and why does the boy refuse?

We will never make the right decisions unless we share an intimate walk with God. It does not come naturally—it is a learned behavior forged through a knowledge of the Word, prayer, and an aversion to compromise.

God's deliverance of Israel is now complete—Midian is totally defeated. Still I feel a bit sad and miss the Gideon we first viewed hiding in the winepress. I yearn for the man who worshiped God and called to his men, "Get up! The Lord has given the Midianite camp into your hands" (Judges 7:15b, NIV). He has changed, and I wonder how he arrived at this place. Could it be the little compromises with sin? The next thing you know we see glimpses of pride, anger, self-interest, ingratitude, and vengefulness in Gideon. That seems to be the way it works when compromise becomes an option in the lives of God's people.

Lately, I have been considering the life of Saul, Israel's first king. He reminds me a bit of Gideon, for he was found hiding among the baggage when he was supposed to be introduced to Israel as king. He started well, but soon fell into a downward spiral making poor decisions and ending dismally. There are countless life lessons to be learned by scrutinizing the life of Saul. Let's spend some time evaluating key decisions that he made that contributed to his downfall.

Week 5 | 112

7. Read these snippets from Saul's life, and record his poor decisions, the subsequent consequences, and any practical application in the life of a Christian.

    1 Samuel 13:5-14

    1 Samuel 15:1-3, 7-29

    1 Samuel 28:4-20

8. Reflect on this sad commentary on the life of Saul in 1 Chronicles 10:13-14. Note your thoughts.

We will never make the right decisions unless we share an intimate walk with God. It does not come naturally–it is a learned behavior forged through a knowledge of the Word, prayer, and an aversion to compromise. I want to end well. Don't you?

Making the right leadership decisions in the moment depends on the character developed over years. [20]
~Jonathan Leeman

WEEK 5 » DAY FIVE » JUDGES 8:22-27

Yesterday in our study, we concentrated our focus on the lives of Gideon and Saul, two men chosen by God to lead the people of Israel. Scripture tells us that both men reluctantly stepped into their positions, but soon began to rely on their own reasoning rather than God's, much to their detriment. Their narratives remind me of the proverb, "There is a way which seems right to a man, but its end is the way of death" (Proverbs 14:12). For Saul, it was a literal death as we discovered yesterday. "So Saul died for his trespass which he committed against the Lord, because of the word of the Lord which he did not keep; and also because he asked counsel of a medium, making inquiry of it, and did not inquire of the Lord. Therefore He killed him and turned the kingdom to David the son of Jesse" (1 Chronicles 10:13-14). God takes disobedience seriously. Gideon, however, has not skidded down that same slippery slope, but seems to be on the precipice, weighing God's way against his own reasoning. So, let's resume our study in chapter 8 to see what happens.

Examine Judges 8:22-27.

1. What request do the men of Israel make of Gideon?

2. Why would you assume that they desired a king?

Tim Keller offers a logical explanation:

> Israel wants to reject God's method of ruling his people. A judge is anointed by him, to deal with the crisis at hand and to lead the people back to living under his rule. But if Gideon says "yes," Israel will have a king appointed by humans, and rule will pass on down to others automatically. Gideon discerns the underlying motive for asking for a king–they want to be ruled by man, not God ... They don't need a king to obey; they need to obey the King they have! [21]

3. How does Gideon reply to their request?

Certainly, Gideon quickly speaks truth to the Israelites. God had designated that they would be a theocracy, a people ruled by Him, in contradistinction to the nations around them. Gideon would not be king. But then the conversation suddenly shifts.

4. What appeal does Gideon make to the people, and what is their response?

The grateful Israelites give generously to Gideon, and he uses the gold to make an ephod, a part of the Old Testament priestly garments.

5. The ephod is described in Exodus 28:4-30. Read the passage to get an accurate idea of the garment. Look for a depiction of the priestly robes in your study Bible or online at biblegateway.com. Make notes of any details you would like to remember.

6. What are the Urim and Thummim, and what are they used for? Use these scriptures to help make your determination.

    Numbers 27:18-21

    1 Samuel 28:5-6

    1 Samuel 30:7-8

Scripture does not inform us what Gideon's motivation is in making the ephod. It is indeed a grave error on his part. Soon the Israelites are worshiping it and totally defying God's commandment, "You shall have no other gods before me. You shall not make for yourself an image in the form of anything in heaven above or on the earth beneath or in the waters below. You shall not bow down to them or worship them" (Exodus 20:3-5a, NIV). In my study, I have read a number of speculations regarding Gideon's motive. Here are a couple of them, so draw your own conclusion.

From *The Books of History* by J. E. Smith:

> In the Old Testament the ephod with its breastpiece is associated with divine revelation. Several times before the battle Gideon had received direct communication from the Lord. Perhaps the ephod was an attempt to continue to receive divine guidance. Did Gideon himself attempt to function as a priest? Was he attempting to establish an alternative channel of divine communication? Did he feel that the normal means of revelation were not adequate? These questions cannot be answered. [22]

From *Be Available* by Warren Wiersbe:

> Whether this ephod was an embellished version of the garment used by the high priest, or some kind of standing idol, we can't tell; but it was used in worship and became a snare to Gideon and the people. Perhaps Gideon used it to determine the will of God and help the people with their problems. If the ephod was indeed a copy of the high priest's garment, then Gideon was definitely out of God's will in duplicating it and using it, because Gideon wasn't a priest. If it was a standing idol, Gideon was disobeying God's Law and corrupting the people as well. It was just a short step from worshiping the ephod to worshiping Baal. [23]

Read Judges 8:28-35 to get a brief synopsis of Gideon's life and the fate of Israel once he died. Worth noting is Gideon's lifestyle which looks markedly similar to that of a king, despite the fact that he has turned down the monarchy.

7. What trappings of kingship do you see in Gideon's life, and what two mistakes does he make according to Deuteronomy 17:17?

Gary Inrig sums up the whole episode like this, "Despite all the achievements of Gideon, he made no permanent spiritual difference in the life of the nation. The worship of the ephod in his own lifetime was judged by God to be spiritual adultery, and, because it was, it led to total apostasy after Gideon's death. Gideon's ephod became his greatest mistake." [24] What a heartbreaking conclusion to a life that could have reformed the future of Israel.

Most of us would become indignant at the mere suggestion that we would worship an idol. Oh, no, we would never do that. The very thought of bowing down to a god made of wood, stone, or metal is simply repulsive to us. Yet, there is a whole culture of idols that in no way resembles that image. Tim Keller in his excellent book, *Counterfeit Gods*, provides a definition, "What is an idol? It is anything more important to you than God, anything that absorbs your heart and imagination more than God, anything you seek to give you what only God can give." [25] He develops this thought further, "A counterfeit god is anything so central and essential to your life that, should you lose it, your life would feel hardly worth living." [26]

Idols can take many forms—success, money, possessions, and people, even exercise, just to name a few. We often see it in others, but do you see it in yourself. Idolatry is an affront to a holy God and its root is sin, the antithesis of holiness. Nancy Leigh DeMoss challenges current thought when she writes, "Somehow, the evangelical world has managed to redefine sin; we have come to view it as normal, acceptable behavior—something perhaps to be tamed or controlled, but not to be eradicated and put to death." [27] God's Word, however, says "Be holy, because I am holy" (1 Peter 1:16b, NIV). DeMoss offers us a timely reminder, "Mark it down—your progress in holiness will never exceed your relationship with the Word of God." [28] Knowing what God expects provides the impetus for holiness.

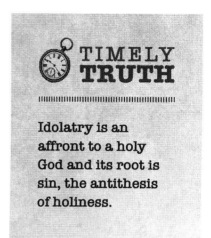

TIMELY TRUTH

Idolatry is an affront to a holy God and its root is sin, the antithesis of holiness.

8. Spend some time in prayer asking the Lord to reveal any idols—anything that is more important to you than Him—and pray for deliverance. Record whatever He reveals to you. Determine with the help of the Holy Spirit to cast down any idol.

Let's close with an excerpt from *Counseling the Hard Cases*:

> Idols are powerful, but two realities cause our hearts to become dissatisfied with idols. The first is that we are created in the image of God and created for God; nothing else will give us eternal purpose or everlasting joy. When we choose to set up a dead, powerless idol and worship at its feet, then we are attended to by a dead, powerless idol that pleases temporarily and superficially. Money disappears. Fame fades away. Children grow up and leave. Our friends fail us. Control is elusive. God alone—in all of His beauty and grace—can promise us joy forever. The second reality that causes our hearts to grow dissatisfied with idols is the grace of God. God is too good to allow His children to worship something or someone that will not satisfy. He is so good that He either wrenches our idols from our hands or makes us miserable as long as we clench and grasp. [29]

If only the Israelites had broken the tie with idols and embraced the One True God.

WEEK 6

When Power Goes to Your Head
Judges 9-10:5

The greatest judgment God can send to His people is to let them have their own way and not interfere.[1]
~Warren Wiersbe

Up until this chapter we have read the accounts of Israel's sin cycle: disobedience, discipline, desperation, and deliverance. Now we have a complete departure from this sequence as we read the story of Abimelech, Gideon's son by his concubine. Abimelech is a man of lowly birth, but grandiose ambitions. He wants the kingship that his father Gideon declined. His rise to power is distinctly different from the heroes of the previous chapters. He is not a judge raised up by the Lord to rescue Israel. He is a king who oppressed Israel, having achieved his rise to the throne through subterfuge and violence.

For forty years Gideon served as a judge in Israel, and the land was undisturbed. "Then it came about, as soon as Gideon was dead, that the sons of Israel again played the harlot with the Baals, and made Baal-berith their god. Thus the sons of Israel did not remember the Lord their God, who had delivered them from the hands of all their enemies on every side; nor did they show kindness to the household of Jerubbaal (that is, Gideon) in accord with all the good that he had done to Israel" (Judges 8:33-35). The children of Israel have short memories and continue to exhibit ungratefulness toward their rescuers and their God. Their short-comings are what open the door for Abimelech's treachery.

The author of Judges writes, "Now Gideon had seventy sons who were his direct descendants, for he had many wives. His concubine who was in Shechem also bore him a son, and he named him Abimelech" (Judges 8:30-31). This reference to Abimelech's ancestry gives us a bit of insight into his psyche. From childhood he had probably been shunned by his half-brothers, making him feel like an outsider. His mother was in Shechem, and it seems his mother's family was more accepting of him than his father's. He was not considered a "direct descendant" of Gideon and did not stand to inherit anything from his father's estate. We can assume Abimelech grew up believing his success in life would rest on his own self-effort and cunning. Blame cannot be solely placed on his childhood circumstances, but these factors would have played a part in shaping the character of this man.

Abimelech's name means my "father is a king." Gideon had refused to establish a dynasty in Israel, recognizing the Lord was their King (see Judges 8:22-23). Abimelech apparently resented his father's decision and considered it a mistake. This fed Abimelech's burning desire to be king. After Gideon dies, Abimelech sees his chance to fulfill his self-proclaimed destiny.

WEEK 6 » DAY ONE » JUDGES 9:1-6

As we have seen over and over, the Israelites refuse to be governed by God. Gary Inrig explains an important principle that applies not only to the Israelites, but to us as well, "...if we reject the true King, we will be ruled by a usurper."[2] As we are about to see, the Israelites' rebellion will deliver them into the hands of a tyrant. Similarly, when we fail to put Christ on the throne of our lives, we become slaves to our sinful nature. As Paul warns in Romans 6:16, "Do you not know that when you present yourselves to someone as slaves for obedience, you are slaves of the one whom you obey, either of sin resulting in death, or of obedience resulting in righteousness?"

Read Judges 9:1-6.

The story of Abimelech takes place in the central part of Israel. Abimelech moved from Ophrah (the home of his father) to Shechem (the home of his mother) in an effort to gather support for his ascent to the throne.

1. Locate Shechem on the map provided on page 7. Since Abimelech is not a judge, you will not find his name on the map. Make a note on the map of the area Abimelech reigned.

Warren Wiersbe writes,

> The Jews had been acquainted with the people of Shechem since the days of the patriarchs (Genesis 12:6; 33:18-20; 34:1). Both Jews and Canaanites lived in Shechem during Abimelech's day, which explains why he started his campaign there. His mother was a Shechemite and his father was a Jew. Therefore, if Abimelech became king, he could represent both constituencies![3]

2. What case does Abimelech present to try to gain support from the leaders in Shechem? (v. 2)

The text does not seem to imply that the seventy sons of Gideon are intent on claiming some type of joint sovereignty over Shechem. Therefore, Abimelech's efforts to garner support from his relatives and the leaders seem to be based on a delusion fed by jealousy. Blinded by ambition and a quest for power, Abimelech is willing to go to any length to secure the throne.

3. How does Abimelech finance his campaign? (v. 4)

Warren Wiersbe notes,

> His accepting money from the Baal worshipers to finance his crusade was a public announcement that he had renounced the God of Israel and was on the side of Baal.[4]

Abimelech aligns himself with Baal, rejecting the God of his fathers. Each of us is required to make a personal decision to either receive or reject Jesus Christ as Savior and Lord. Receiving Him puts us in right relationship with God the Father, forgives our sin debt, empowers us for living through the indwelling Holy Spirit, and assures us of eternity in Heaven with Jesus. In Joshua's farewell address to the children of Israel, he said, "Choose for yourselves today whom you will serve: whether the gods which your fathers served which were beyond the River, or the gods of the Amorites in whose land you are living, but as for me and my house, we will serve the Lord" (Joshua 24:15). Joshua chose to follow the Lord. Abimelech made his decision to reject the Lord and his fate was sealed. Who have you chosen to follow? As for me and my house, we decided to follow Jesus back in 1978 and He has never failed us yet! He is a faithful King!

4. With his support and financial backing in place, what does Abimelech do next? (vv. 4-5)

Using deception or cunning, Abimelech and his band of cutthroats manage to get the upper hand on his half-brothers, capturing and killing them all execution-style "on one stone." Only the youngest, Jotham, escapes the bloodletting by hiding. There seems no reason for Abimelech to murder them other than revenge, most likely stemming from his feelings of rejection (whether real or perceived) as the illegitimate son of Gideon.

Wiersbe provides additional insight,

> Why didn't somebody stop these murderers and defend Gideon's family? Because the people of Israel had forgotten both the goodness of the Lord and the kindness of Gideon (Judges 8:33–35). They had neither the conviction to be concerned nor the courage to intervene.[5]

God's people have once again forgotten Him.

Judges 9:6 tells us that "All the men of Shechem and all Beth-millo assembled together and made Abimelech king." There is no indication that Abimelech's rule ever reached beyond the regions of Shechem. He becomes the king of a city-state, although he surely has far greater ambitions.

5. Where does Abimelech's coronation take place? (v. 6)

This is probably the "oak of Moreh" (see Genesis 12:6) where the Lord appeared to Abraham and promised the land of Canaan to his descendants. It was near the site where the children of Israel heard the blessings and curses read from the Law and committed to obey (see Deuteronomy 11:26-32; Joshua 8:30-35). Here Jacob buried the idols when he called his family back to the one true God (see Genesis 35:1-5). And this is most likely the location where Joshua gave his farewell address, admonishing them to choose to obey the Lord (see Joshua 24:1-26). So much of the sacred history of the nation of Israel was tied to this consecrated place. Abimelech desecrates this historical and holy site when he takes the crown, acquired by mayhem and murder.

Dark times ruled by a murderous, unethical, and ungodly king. Certainly, the sons of Israel deserve such a leader because they continually "forsook the Lord and served Baal and the Ashtaroth" (Judges 2:13). We would wholeheartedly give our consent for God to wipe them out from the face of the earth and feel justified in our judgmental attitude were it not for the conviction we have experienced as we read of Israel's unfaithfulness towards her God.

Like Israel, we are prone to worship and serve idols of our own making. How grateful we are for the promise of our Faithful King to acknowledge our broken and contrite spirits when we confess our sins. We are thankful for God's patience with us, all the while we are often stingy when required to exhibit patience to those in need of ours. We tend to begrudge offering forgiveness to others, while relishing it when it is offered to us. May we remember that we too are broken people. Were it not for God, our Faithful King, we would perish in the way!

WEEK 6 » DAY TWO » JUDGES 9:7-21

Jotham, Gideon's youngest son, is able to escape the carnage at Ophrah and hide from Abimelech's mercenaries. Having heard of Abimelech's impending coronation, Jotham "went and stood on the top of Mount Gerizim, and lifted his voice and called out" (Judges 9:7). This natural platform provides excellent acoustics so his voice can project to those below. His vantage point will also allow him to escape easily should it become necessary.

Using my sanctified imagination, I can envision the scene. The crowd presses in to catch a glimpse of their new king, unfazed by the murderous circumstances that propelled him to this position. The high priest from the house of Baal-berith deftly lifts the crown from an embroidered velvet cushion trimmed with gold tassels presented by a young boy who serves at the temple. Savoring the moment, the high priest hoists the crown into the air with a flourish. Abimelech bows low and kneels reverently. The priest holds the crown aloft for a moment in order to provide a bit of drama and accentuate the importance of the event. The crowd draws a collective breath and leans in to catch every nuance of this momentous occasion. At just the right moment, Jotham interrupts the ceremony and calls out, "Listen to me, O men of Shechem, that God may listen to you" (Judges 9:7).

Jotham proceeds to deliver a parable in hopes the men of Shechem will realize the foolishness of making Abimelech their king. His parable is the first one recorded in Scripture. We typically attach the use of parables to the earthly ministry of our Lord and rightly so, but He was not the first to incorporate their use as a way of revealing a deeper message of truth. In his story, Jotham personifies inanimate objects (trees) to make his point. The purpose of his story is to call the people of Shechem to account before the Lord for accepting the corrupt murderer, Abimelech, as their king.

Read Judges 9:7-21.

1. Summarize Jotham's parable in verses 7-15.

Jotham's parable pictures trees looking for a king. They approach the olive tree with its valuable oil, the fig tree with its tasty fruit, and the vine with its clusters used to make new wine. Each tree, considered a candidate for a king, has great intrinsic value and produces a valuable commodity for the people. Each refuses to leave the function for which they were created to fulfill to accept the role of king.

Only the bramble remains. Out of desperation the trees ask the bramble to reign as their king. The bramble replies, "If in truth you are anointing me as king over you, come and take refuge in my shade" (Judges 9:15). Jotham interjects extreme irony at this point in the story. The bramble was a noxious thorn-bush that grows close to the ground and could hardly offer shade to a towering tree. Its only use was as kindling to start fires for cooking. Furthermore, during the dry season, wildfires would often break out in bramble bushes, posing a genuine threat to crops and livestock. Appointing such an inept bramble to be king over the majestic trees implies a potential result–fire that would "consume the cedars of Lebanon" (Judges 9:15).

Jotham makes application of the parable. Abimelech is the "bramble king" installed despite his lack of experience, his villainous character, and his possible delusional personality. Their choice of Abimelech indicates their lack of integrity and discredited Gideon's memory and his courageous fight on their behalf. Perhaps the most telling seems to be that they absolve Abimelech from his murderous rampage against his family members in order to ensure his reign.

Wiersbe concludes,

> The men of Shechem should have been ashamed of the way they rejected the house of Gideon and honored a worthless opportunist like Abimelech. Eventually, both Abimelech and his followers would destroy one another. Abimelech considered himself to be a stately tree of great value, but Jotham said he was nothing but a useless weed. What a blow to the new king's pride! When they chose Abimelech as their king, the men of Shechem didn't get useful olive oil, tasty figs, or cheery wine; they got only thorns–fuel for the fire.[6]

Jotham presses the claims of his father's bravery on their behalf, "My father fought for you and risked his life and delivered you from the hand of Midian; but you have risen against my father's house today and have killed his sons, seventy men, on one stone, and have made Abimelech, the son of his maidservant, king over the men of Shechem, because he is your relative" (Judges 9:17-18). Jotham credits the murder of his brothers to the citizens of Shechem because they had financed Abimelech's barbaric insurrection with funds from their temple of Baal. He also accuses them of partisanship because Abimelech was one of their own.

Jotham gives a solemn warning to the leaders in Shechem, "If then you have dealt in truth and integrity with Jerubbaal and his house this day, rejoice in Abimelech, and let him also rejoice in you" (Judges 9:19). If the Shechemites believe their treachery against the house of Gideon is just, then they can be confident in the choice they have made. "But if not, let fire come out from Abimelech and consume the men of Shechem and Beth-millo; and let fire come out from the men of Shechem and from Beth-millo, and consume Abimelech" (Judges 9:20). If not, instead of providing strength and leadership, Abimelech would prove to be the kindling with which Shechem would be consumed.

Skip ahead and read Judges 9:57.

2. What ultimately happens to the men of Shechem?

3. How are the words Jotham delivers at Abimelech's coronation described in this verse?

Judges 9:21 tells us, "Then Jotham escaped and fled." Obviously, the Shechemites are not receptive to Jotham's rebuke and he is forced into hiding because of his brother, Abimelech.

Dark times. Abimelech has garnered support by misrepresenting his brothers' intentions. He has financed his campaign with money dedicated to Baal. He has eliminated any threats to his reign by executing all of his half-brothers except Jotham, who escapes the horrendously deviant plot. Dark times indeed.

WEEK 6 » DAY THREE » JUDGES 9:22-41

Read Judges 9:22-41.

1. How long does Abimelech rule Israel? (v. 22)

Considering the methods he has employed to gain his leadership role, we can assume he was willing to continue to use deception, cruelty, and violence to maintain it. Sadly, it appears Abimelech has not repented and returned to God. Adding idol worship to his list of offenses, we can only imagine the impact of the ungodly leadership he provides and the role he plays in leading his people further from the one true God. Proverbs 29:2 says, "When the righteous increase, the people rejoice, but when a wicked man rules, people groan." His is not the reign of a monarch but simply that of a tyrant, considering the savagery he uses to gain control.

Should we consider the fact Abimelech was allowed to reign as an endorsement by the Lord? Certainly not! Abimelech's story highlights both the patience of God as well as the judgment of God.

God desires for everyone to come to the saving knowledge of Jesus Christ.

2. Look up 1 Timothy 2:3-4. I often pray this passage for those lost friends and family members on my prayer list. Consider adding it to yours. What does this passage teach us?

3. This same truth is restated in 2 Peter 3:9. What does this verse teach us about the Lord?

God gives Abimelech the space of three years to repent. Can you imagine what the impact would have been on his kingdom had he "turned to God from idols to serve a living and true God" (1 Thessalonians 1:9)? As Warren Wiersbe cautions, "God is a patient God, but God is holy. Do not misinterpret God's patience as His indifference to sin."[7] His holiness requires justice. Judgement will come on those who reject Him. Just rewards may or may not be meted out on the unrighteous on this earth, but damnation and eternal separation await those who reject Jesus Christ as Lord and Savior.

4. What is the first obstacle Abimelech faces in his leadership? (vv. 23-25)

Just three years earlier, Abimelech and his allies had joined forces to eliminate his only viable threat to his rise to power in Shechem. Now, his former co-conspirators have banded together to do the same to him.

The writer clearly wants his readers to notice that the downfall and destruction of Abimelech and the men of Shechem is divine retribution for slaughtering the seventy sons of Gideon. Although the youngest brother, Jotham, manages to escape with his life, bringing the total slaughtered by the hand of Abimelech to sixty nine, he is included in the number of seventy deaths held against Abimelech and his supporters (see Judges 9:5; 18; 23; 56). The intent of Abimelech's heart was to kill all seventy of his brothers. Therefore, his youngest brother's death is counted among those massacred. Proverbs 23:7 says, "For as [a man] thinks within himself, so he is."

The tide of Abimelech's popularity quickly turns against him, so much so that the Shechemites begin to work against the king. They set up ambushes in the mountain passes to loot caravans that traveled on nearby trade routes. The activities of these bandits rob the coffers of Abimelech of tolls and taxes, money he considers to be his. All of this is designed to destabilize the economy and strike fear in the community. Perhaps the hope was that Abimelech himself would respond to the threat with a personal confrontation, giving them an opportunity to assassinate him.

5. A new rival to Abimelech's jurisdiction is introduced in verse 26. Who is he and how does he attempt to win over the loyalties of the men of Shechem? (vv. 26-27)

6. Who is Zebul? (v. 30)

Abimelech is an "absentee king" for the people of Shechem. His headquarters are in Arumah (see Judges 9:41), and he has appointed Zebul to rule in Shechem.

7. When Zebul reports Gaal's sedition to Abimelech, what happens next? (vv. 34-41)

Based on Zebul's intel and military strategy, Abimelech wins a decisive victory over Gaal and his insurgents. Abimelech, with his visions of grandeur, has no idea his reign and his life are about to come to an abrupt and gruesome ending.

I am reminded of the parable Jesus told about a wealthy man who trusted in his riches. He was making plans to build large barns and storehouses to accommodate his rapidly increasing bottom line. He said to himself, " 'Soul, you have many goods laid up for many years to come; take your ease, eat, drink, and be merry.' But God said to him, 'You fool! This very night your soul is required of you; and now who will own what you have prepared?' So is the man who stores up treasure for himself, and is not rich toward God" (Luke 12:19-21). May we be careful to "store up for [ourselves] treasures in heaven, where neither moth nor rust destroys, and where thieves do not break in or steal" (Matthew 6:20). Living in dark times among broken people, may we get a fresh vision of eternity, prepared for us, by our Faithful King!

WEEK 6 » DAY FOUR » JUDGES 9:42-57

As we ended yesterday, Gaal and his relatives have been driven out of Shechem, but apparently some of the forces, intent on overthrowing Abimelech, remain encamped in the field.

Before moving on, I want to draw some insight from this narrative. The enemy was displaced, but not completely routed. As believers, we have an enemy and we are continually engaged in spiritual warfare. Satan, "the prince of the power of the air" (Ephesians 2:2), heads a well-trained, highly-organized demon army who is intent on enticing us to sin, sending us spiraling into defeat, despair, and (quite possibly) full-blown depression in order to spoil our testimony for Christ.

1. Read Ephesians 6:10-17. How does Paul describe Satan's army?

We are up against a formidable foe, but fear not, beloved! God has provided weapons through the full armor of God. He has also given us a divine military strategy.

2. Read 2 Corinthians 10:3-5. Describe our weapons and our battle plan.

3. How do we lay hold of our divinely powerful weapons?

4. Are you prepared to fight? What is hindering you from getting into the battle?

Now, back to our story.

Read Judges 9:42-57.

The rebellion led by Gaal had been put down, but Abimelech seems to have spent the night brooding over the rebellion. Although many of Gaal's followers were mortally wounded, Abimelech's wrath is not fully satisfied. The revolt has stirred up in Abimelech feelings of revenge against all his constituents. He returns to Shechem for the second stage of the battle, full of rage and bloodlust.

5. What tactics does Abimelech use to overthrow Shechem? (vv. 42-45)

When the leaders of Shechem hear about Abimelech's deadly rampage against the inhabitants of Shechem, they gather in the inner chamber of the outlying tower of Shechem which is adjoined to the temple of El-berith.

6. What do Abimelech and his men do when they get to the tower? (vv. 48-49)

Abimelech then moves on to Thebez, a city that has apparently joined the rebellion against him. The city is unfortified, with only a strong tower in the center of it to offer protection. Judges 9:51 explains what happens next, "All the men and women with all the leaders of the city fled there and shut themselves in; and they went up on the roof of the tower."

7. What happens when Abimelech approaches the entrance of the tower? (v. 53)

8. What is Abimelech's biggest concern as he is dying? (v. 54)

Wiersbe explains that Abimelech experienced a three-fold humiliation:

> (1) He was killed, but not really in a battle; (2) he was killed by a woman, which was a disgrace to a soldier; and (3) he was killed with a millstone, not a sword. The fact that his armor-bearer finished the job with a sword didn't change anything; for centuries later, Abimelech's shameful death was remembered as being accomplished by a woman (2 Samuel 11:21).[8]

The writer emphatically attributes the deaths of Abimelech and the men of Shechem to divine retribution lest the reader overlooks the obvious. "Thus God repaid the wickedness of Abimelech, which he had done to his father in killing his seventy brothers" (Judges 9:56). Abimelech loses his life and the kingdom he has so violently seized. Concerning a worthless wicked man, the Bible says, "His calamity will come suddenly; instantly he will be broken and there will be no healing" (Proverbs 6:15).

God also "returned all the wickedness of the men of Shechem on their heads" (Judges 9:57). The curse pronounced by Jotham was realized. As Longfellow writes, "Though the mills of God grind slowly, yet they grind exceeding small."[9]

No bloodshed ever goes unnoticed by the Lord. No injustice will be left unpunished. He is "the Judge of all the earth" and He will "deal justly" (Genesis 18:25). In Deuteronomy 32:35, the Bible says, "Vengeance is Mine, and retribution, in due time their foot will slip; for the day of their calamity is near, and the impending things are hastening upon them." While we cannot understand the ways of God (see Isaiah 55:8-9), we can rest in the truth that "no purpose of [His] can be thwarted" (Job 42:2). God is patient towards repentance, but sure in regard to judgment. Galatians 6:7-8 says, "Do not be deceived, God is not mocked; for whatever a man sows, this he will also reap. For the one who sows to his own flesh will from the flesh reap corruption, but the one who sows to the Spirit will from the Spirit reap eternal life." Even in dark times, our God is our Faithful King. By faith, we can trust He will fulfill His plans and purposes.

WEEK 6 » DAY FIVE » JUDGES 10:1-5

Following Abimelech's disastrous rule, God raises up two faithful judges. The psalmist writes, "For not from the east, nor from the west, nor from the desert comes exaltation; but God is the Judge; He puts down one and exalts another" (Psalm 75:6-7). What is unique about these two judges is the fact that these men serve Israel apart from her previously noted sin cycle–rebellion, retribution, repentance, redemption, and rest.

Read Judges 10:1-5.

Keller shares,

> This is the sheer grace of God. The people have completely abandoned him. They have opted to be led by a man who was not chosen by the Lord, but by himself, who was recommended not by the Lord's divine commission but by his own power. Israel has sunk to the depths and they are not even crying out in repentance, yet God sends them Tola and Jair to be judge-saviors they are not asking for.[10]

1. After Abimelech dies, who are the next two judges God raises up to save Israel? (v. 1)

2. On the chart on page 11, fill in the details we learn about Tola and Jair.

Little is written concerning Tola and Jair, but the fact Israel enjoys peace and security under their leadership for 45 years suggests they were faithful men of God. What Israel needs at this time is stable and reliable leadership, and it appears both of these judges fill this role.

3. The areas where Tola and Jair govern are indicated on the map on page 7. Note the regions where they served as judges to Israel.

God gives Israel peace and prosperity for 45 years. During this season of rest, we would expect great strides in spiritual growth and discipleship in Israel. Sadly, temporary reformation rather than genuine repentance seems to be the norm for God's people. If only Israel had responded properly to God, revival would have been the long-term result. As we will see next week, following the death of Jair, the nation "forsook the Lord and did not serve Him" (Judges 10:6). How quickly they forgot about the Lord and the people who had served them faithfully!

One of my favorite spiritual principles, and one that I have applied to my own faith-walk many times, is tucked in Genesis 41:1-37. Read this passage.

4. Describe Pharaoh's dream.

5. Pharaoh sent for Joseph to interrupt his troubling dream. What was Joseph's interpretation and his conclusion to its meaning?

Don't miss this great truth! During seasons of peace and prosperity, we need to fill our barns in preparation for difficult days, which will come to all of us. This includes applying God's wisdom to financial windfalls and other practical matters of life as well as our spiritual lives. God gives us seasons of respite and rest. During those seasons, we need to fill up our spiritual barns with truth from God's Word, rather than coasting and relying on our spiritual residue. These stored-up truths will carry us during those times of famine, such as a health crisis, wayward children, caring for aging parents, death of a loved one, etc. In these watershed moments, we need God's Word hidden in our hearts to carry us through dark times.

If we have been careless in the seasons of ease, we will be powerless in the seasons of stress, with little or no working knowledge of the Scripture to sustain us and few opportunities to feast (spend extended time with the Lord) on His Word.

Of the virtuous woman, Proverbs 31:18 says, "Her lamp does not go out at night." She provides light in the nighttime in her home because during the daylight hours she put oil in her lamp. She prepares in the daylight for the anticipated times of darkness to come. Again, Proverbs 31:25 says, "Strength and dignity are her clothing, and she smiles at the future." The future is no threat to this godly woman. She is clothed in the Lord, and she has prepared for seasons of need during the seasons of plenty. Therefore, she smiles at the future, her earthbound one and her eternal one in glory with the Savior. "Charm is deceitful and beauty is vain, but a woman who fears the Lord, she shall be praised" (Proverbs 31:30).

Beloved, get busy filling up your barns and store up God's Word in your heart. This is wisdom! Just as in the book of Judges, we are living in dark times among broken people. Fear not, for we serve Heaven's Faithful King!

WEEK 7

When You Speak Before You Think
Judges 10:6 – 12:15

This is our time on the history line of God. This is it.
What will we do with the one deep exhale of God on this earth?
For we are but a vapor and we have to make it count.
We're on. Direct us, Lord, and get us on our feet.[1]
~Beth Moore

As we continue our study through the redemptive period of the judges, we are becoming acquainted with a people who remind us, sadly, of ourselves. After the death of Gideon and the end of the reign of terror brought upon Israel by his son, Abimelech, the people of Israel enjoy a number of years of peace and prosperity. However, once again prosperity leads the Israelites into complacency that spirals into unbelief and winds up with God's people being enticed to worship false gods. As John Calvin notes, "Men are undoubtedly more in danger from prosperity than from adversity. For when matters go smoothly, they flatter themselves and are intoxicated by their success."[2]

Just like the Israelites, we live in a time when we are surrounded by pagan temptations and find it easy to succumb to the danger of prosperity. Too often, lesser things rise above our devotion to Christ. And the plummet we take into idolatry always costs us far more than we ever thought we would have to pay.

This is our time on the history line of God. This is it. This. Is. It.

At the end of our lives, we will be known for five things. Our character, who we are. Our conduct, how we act. Our conversation, what we say. Our creed, what we believe. Our contribution, what we leave behind.

What are you doing with your time on the history line of God?

Are you all in?

Or have peace and prosperity lulled you into complacency, indifference, or worse?

Keep those questions open in your heart and mind throughout this week. Allow God to chisel away at your character, your conduct, your conversation, and your creed to the point that you are shaped into a closer resemblance of God Himself and ask Him to mold your contribution into a kingdom legacy for His glory.

WEEK 7 » DAY ONE » JUDGES 10:6-18

Read Judges 10:6-18.

Our passage today opens with words that are sadly familiar, "Then the sons of Israel again did evil in the sight of the Lord." As you walk through Judges 10:6-12:15 this week, notate the verses that correspond to each segment in the sin cycle.

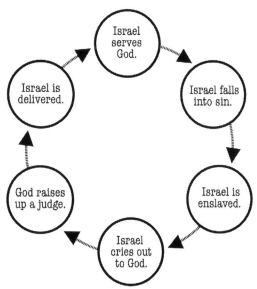

Israel has reached a new low. Not only have God's people once again turned from Jehovah God and fallen into idol worship, but they are worshiping multiple deities.

1. Make a list of the pagan gods that the Israelites are worshiping.

    • The _____ and the _____.

    • The gods of _____.

    • The gods of _____.

    • The gods of _____.

    • The gods of _____.

    • The gods of _____.

Tim Keller writes,

> The Baals and the Ashtoreths were the gods of the "native" Canaanites. But the gods of Aram (to the northwest) and Sidon (to the north), or Ammon and Moab (to the east) and the Philistines (to the south), belonged to peoples outside of Canaan who often came into Canaan and oppressed the Israelites.[3]

God has already delivered His people from seven different nations (Judges 10:11-12), but now they have been theologically seduced by seven different false gods...the gods of their defeated enemies! It is no wonder that God is angry with them. Were it not for God's faithfulness to His covenant, Israel would be no more.

2. How is God's anger described in 10:7?

3. How does God punish the Israelites for their apostasy, turning their backs on Him?

When you sell a possession, the new owner can do with that object whatever he or she pleases. Such is the case when God "sells" the Israelites to the Philistines and the Ammonites. God removes His protection and gives them over to a double oppression from the two nations whose gods they are serving.

Read Romans 1:21-25.

In these verses, Paul writes about the devastating consequences of idolatry.

4. How is their idolatry described?

5. What is God's judgment on those who worship other gods?

The Greek word for "lusts" is *epithumia* which means "an overwhelming drive, an enslaving, uncontrollable desire."[4] In short, they will become slaves to their idolatry. Ed Welch writes, "Either we will love and serve God, or we will love and serve our idols. Idols exist in our lives because we love them and invite them in. But once idols find a home, they are unruly and resist leaving. In fact, they change from being the servants of our desires to being our masters."[5]

6. What is a present day example of idolatry leading to enslavement?

The Israelites again find out that idolatry is long on promise, but short on delivery. The idols they are worshipping promise freedom, pleasure, and prosperity, but deliver slavery, shame, and death.

7. What words does the writer of Judges use to describe the severity of the suffering the Israelites experienced during their oppression? (Judges 10:8-9)

So after 18 years of suffering at the hands of the Ammonites, it finally occurs to the Israelites that their false gods are useless and they cry out to Jehovah for deliverance.

8. What is God's piercing rebuke to their cry for help? (vv. 11-14)

God is not impressed with their so-called "repentance". He has seen their temporary change of heart before. Essentially, Israel has developed a pattern of using God as a "get out of jail free card" when they regret the consequences of their sin, but are not repentant for their sin. They feel remorse, but they are not repentant.

They want relief. They want a rescue. But God wants a relationship. And so, He is willing to wait until His people quit placing their hopes in other gods.

9. What words and actions demonstrate that the Israelites are truly repenting from their idol worship? (vv. 15-16)

10. God then responds to their genuine repentance because "He could bear the misery of Israel no longer." As you read those words, what are your thoughts about the faithfulness of God?

What a magnificent display of the grace and mercy of God and the depth of His love for Israel! Adam Clarke writes,

> What a proof of the philanthropy of God! Here His compassion moved on a small scale, but it was the same principle that led Him to give His Son Jesus Christ to be a sacrifice for the sins of the whole world. God grieves for the miseries to which His creatures are reduced by their own sins.[6]

Here, we see the tension between the holiness of God and His mercy toward His people. This struggle will continue throughout the Old Testament and not be resolved until Calvary when God "being rich in mercy, because of His great love with which He loved us, even when we were dead in our transgressions, made us alive together with Christ (by grace you have been saved), and raised us up with Him, and seated us with Him in the heavenly *places* in Christ Jesus, so that in the ages to come He might show the surpassing riches of His grace in kindness toward us in Christ Jesus" (Ephesians 2:4-7).

As we read in Judges 10:17-18, war is imminent. The Ammonites are gathered in Gilead and are gearing up for battle. The Israelites respond by assembling at Mizpah, also in Gilead. The leaders of Gilead caucus to look for a volunteer to lead their army. As we will see tomorrow, God's next deliverer is about to arrive.

Throughout today's study, you may have found yourself shaming the Israelites for their recurring idolatry. But before you go too far down that path, take a moment to consider John Calvin's pointed statement, "Man's nature, so to speak, is a perpetual factory of idols."[7] Although it may make you uncomfortable, ask yourself, "Is there anything or anyone that I have elevated above God?"

The idols in our lives are mesmerizing mirages that expose our fatal tendency to worship lesser things. Whether it is a possession, a habit, a dream, or a person, anytime we attach our God-sized longings to something other than Him, we succumb to idolatry. Idol worship hijacks us from our original intended purpose—to worship our Creator. We must forsake our pursuit of the lesser things and cultivate a high view of God to which our only response will be an all-of-life abandon to the supreme worth of God's enoughness.

TIMELY TRUTH

We must forsake our pursuit of the lesser things and cultivate a high view of God to which our only response will be an all-of-life abandon to the supreme worth of God's enoughness.

You must not have any other god but me. You must not make for yourself an idol of any kind or an image of anything in the heavens or on the earth or in the sea. You must not bow down to them or worship them, for I, the Lord your God, am a jealous God who will not tolerate your affection for any other gods.
Exodus 20:3-5a, NLT

WEEK 7 » DAY TWO » JUDGES 11:1-28

It has well been said, "everything rises and falls on leadership." Never is that statement more true than when a nation is at war. On September 3, 1939, Britain responded to mounting German aggression by declaring war. Under the leadership of Neville Chamberlin, Britain joined forces with France and adopted a defensive posture, waiting for Germany to make its next move. When Germany invaded Norway, the Allies were slow to respond, outnumbered, and had to withdraw from Norway, leaving the country in the hands of the Nazis. At that point, Chamberlin's ability to lead was called into account and the search for a wartime leader led Parliament to the man who would courageously lead the country through the war–Winston Churchill.

In hindsight, it is difficult to imagine the outcome of World War II without Churchill's leadership, but his was an unlikely rise to power. Earlier military failures and his unpopular opinions about Germany had banished Churchill into a political wilderness for a number of years before the war. However, those difficult years only strengthened his resolve and prepared him to lead during a pivotal moment in history. As Seth Godin observes, "Leadership is a gradual process, one where you take responsibility years before you are given authority."[8] After mounting pressure from the British people, Parliament formed a National Government and Churchill was asked to be the Prime Minister on May 10, 1940. His passionate speeches and resolute leadership during the London Blitz held the besieged nation together, while his bulldog tenacity and unwavering sense of conviction rallied the Allies to victory against Hitler's Germany in 1945 and literally altered the course of history.

Similarly, Jephthah, the next leader of Israel is not a likely choice. In fact, at first glance, his disqualifications for leadership outnumber his qualifications. Born into a dysfunctional family, Jephthah lacks the formal training and pedigree typically associated with becoming a head of state, yet God raises him up to be just that. It is Jephthah's time on the history line of God.

Read Judges 11:1-28.

1. Make notes on the biographical information you learn about Jephthah in verses 1-3.

After he is rejected by his family, Jepthah flees to Tob, an area most commentators believe was located in a desolate location about 15 miles to the east-north-east of Ramoth-gilead just outside the eastern boundary of Israel (modern day Syria).[9]

When the leaders of Gilead go to Tob to approach Jephthah about becoming their military leader, their basic request is, "We have a problem, can you fix it for us?"

2. What is Jephthah's initial response? (vv. 6-8)

3. When the leaders ask Jephthah a second time, upon what condition does he accept the judgeship? (vv. 9-11)

There is a similar pattern with the exchange between Jephthah and the leaders from Gilead and the Israelites' dialogue with God that we saw yesterday in Judges 10:10-16. The way God's people are treating the person God has chosen to be their next judge is they same way they are treating God.

Jephthah finds himself in a place where he can negotiate a good deal to gain the honor and significance his family has denied him. After he agrees to lead Israel, Jephthah and the elders of Gilead travel to Mizpah to ratify their agreement before the Lord. Mizpah is the same place where Laban and Jacob made their covenant and set up memorial stones as a witness (Genesis 31:43-50). The word, *mizpah* means "watchtower" and the idea is "If you go back on your word, God will see and may He punish you."[10]

Before we go further, pause for a moment and consider Jephthah's preparation for leadership during his time in the Tob wilderness. Moses, David, Elijah, and Paul all had similar wilderness experiences.

4. In what ways do you think Jephthah's wilderness time would have prepared him to lead the Israelites?

5. Think about a wilderness time in your life where you can now look back and see that God was using that time to prepare you for the next thing He had for you. What are some ways God has used that time of preparation in your life?

Although Jephthah is fully capable of leading the Israelites to war against the Ammonites, he first tries to use words and his ability to negotiate a peaceful resolution with the Ammonites.

6. When Jephthah sends a delegation to negotiate with the king of the Ammonites, why does the king say he is waging war against Israel? (vv. 12-13)

The king of Ammon is convinced that the Jews, under the leadership of Moses, had stolen land from the Ammonites. He is seeking to settle an old score and makes it clear that the only way to avoid war is for Israel to give back the land.

7. Look at the map on page 7 and mark the area bordered by the Jabbok River running north to the Arnon River (a distance of approximately 50 miles) and eastward from the Jordan River for about 20 miles that the king of Ammon asserts belongs to his nation.

In verses 14-27, Jephthah refutes the king's claim to the land with a four-point argument. First, Jephthah sets the record straight from a **historical** perspective. In verses 15-22, he recounts the way Israel came into possession of the land east of the Jordan River.

8. Read Numbers 21:21-35 and take notes on the events that led to Israel acquiring the land in question. (Note how these verses correspond with Jephthah's history lesson.)

Jephthah corrects the king's attempt to rewrite history by explaining that Israel took the land from the Amorites, not the Ammonites. In fact, in Deuteronomy 2:19, God had forbidden the Israelites to take land from the Ammonites, "When you come to the Ammonites, do not harass them or provoke them to war, for I will not give you possession of any land belonging to the Ammonites. I have given it as a possession to the descendants of Lot" (NIV) and as Moses explained in Deuteronomy 2:37, they obeyed God's instructions, "However, we avoided the land of the Ammonites all along the Jabbok River and the towns in the hill country–all the places the LORD our God had commanded us to leave alone" (NLT).

The second argument Jephthah makes is **theological** (vv. 23-24). Jephthah explains that God gave the Israelites the land and that the Ammonites should be content with the land one of their gods, Chemosh, has given to them.

Jephthah's third line of defense is a **rational** argument. In verse 25, he counters that if Balak, the king of Moab did not think it wise to attack Israel, then perhaps the king of Ammon should learn from his example.

The fourth argument Jephthah gives is **chronological** based upon the time Israel has possessed the land.

9. How long has Israel lived on the east of the Jordan River? (v. 26)

Jephthah concludes his case by asking why Ammon has not attempted to take the land centuries before now and then in his final statement he asserts, "'I therefore have not sinned against you, but you are doing me wrong by making war against me; may the LORD, the Judge, judge today between the sons of Israel and the sons of Ammon'" (Judges 11:24). Up to this point in their history, eight different judges have led Israel. To his credit, Jephthah recognizes that God is the true Judge, the only One who is able to lead His people and conquer their enemies.

10. How does the king of Ammon respond to the argument that Jephthah has presented to him? (v. 28)

11. Read Daniel 4:34-35 and Luke 1:51-53. How do these verses on the sovereignty of God encourage you in a situation you are facing?

> *While it looks like things are out of control, behind the scenes
> there is a God Who hasn't surrendered His authority.*[11]
> ~A.W. Tozer

WEEK 7 » DAY THREE » JUDGES 11:29-40

Up to this time in his story, Jephthah has demonstrated godly leadership.

- He is willing to forgive those who have previously rejected him and come to their rescue (Judges 11:1-11).

- He has proclaimed God's faithfulness to His people (Judges 11:15-28).

- He has acknowledged that God is the ultimate Judge (Judges 11:27).

After the king of Ammon rebuffs Jephthah's arguments, it becomes obvious that an attack from the Ammonites is eminent and Jephthah has no recourse other than to fight. However, he is not left to contend with the enemy in his own strength. The Spirit of the Lord comes upon Jephthah (11:29) and energizes him for the battle ahead.

When God calls someone to serve Him, He will equip that person for the task. Paul, who also had an unfavorable past, gives thanks to God for enabling him to do what God had called him to do:

> I thank Christ Jesus our Lord, who has strengthened me, because He considered me faithful, putting me into service, even though I was formerly a blasphemer and a persecutor and a violent aggressor. Yet I was shown mercy because I acted ignorantly in unbelief; and the grace of our Lord was more than abundant, with the faith and love which are found in Christ Jesus. I Timothy 1:12-14

1. Take a moment to consider the work God has called you (or is calling you) to do. (And if you are still taking in breath, He has work for you to do.)

    - What specifically has God placed in your heart to do?

    - Are you totally dependent upon Him to accomplish the task or are you trying to contend in your own strength?

    - Like Jephthah, are you facing a battle?

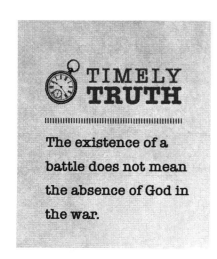

TIMELY TRUTH

The existence of a battle does not mean the absence of God in the war.

The existence of a battle does not mean the absence of God in the war. When we are in a battle, we must fight the good fight of faith (1 Timothy 6:12), being confident that He will work out all things for our good (Romans 8:28) even when we face opposition. Stand on the promise of God's Word that the "God who started this great work in you [will] keep at it and bring it to a flourishing finish on the very day Christ Jesus appears" (Philippians 1:6, MSG). Because it is always too soon to give in!

Jephthah, strengthened by the Spirit for the work God has for him, is poised to lead the Israelites to victory. And then we get to Judges 11:30-31.

2. What vow does Jephthah make? (vv. 30-31)

Even though the Spirit of the Lord has come upon him with power, Jephthah falls back on his own strength, his ability to use words to get what he wants. He approaches the Lord the same way he did the Israelite leaders and the Ammonite king. He tries to negotiate with Him by making a hasty, condition-based and carelessly worded vow. (If you are like me, about right now you are wondering exactly what Jephthah is thinking.)

3. What do Proverbs 20:25 and Ecclesiastes 5:2-5 warn about making a rash vow?

It was acceptable for the Jews to make a vow to God as long as they obeyed the laws He had given regarding vows (Numbers 30:1-2, Deuteronomy 23:21-23). However, Jephthah's vow was an impulsive attempt to bargain victory. F.B. Meyer notes, "There is no need to bribe God's help, as Jephthah did, by his rash promise. He will give gladly and freely out of His own heart of love the help and deliverance we need, if only our cause is rightly ordered before Him."[12] Jephthah's vow about the upcoming battle is unnecessary because his cause is just and he has already been empowered by the Spirit. Promises like Jephthah's, made to try to manipulate God or to try to persuade Him to do what we want Him to do, are foolish. To speak in such a way to the Almighty is to view Him as One who has the power to give, but will not do so without receiving something in return. Consequently, we feel obliged to bargain with Him to get what we want.

With an army that was more than likely quite a bit smaller than the enemy's militia, Jephthah engages the Ammonites in battle and "the LORD [gives] them into his hand" (11:32) in a decisive victory over the enemy that has oppressed

Israel for the past eighteen years. So Jephthah returns home to Mizpah, the victorious new judge of Israel in what should be a time of celebration over what God has done. But, that is when Jephthah's vow hits him like a ton of bricks.

4. Who is the first one to come out of the door of Jephthah's house? (v. 34)

You can hear the excruciating pain in Jephthah's voice when he cries "Alas" as his only daughter comes out of his front door dancing in joy at her hero father's victorious return home and he recalls the vow he has made.

5. When Jephthah tells his daughter about the tragic vow he has made, how does she respond? (vv. 35-37)

6. What do Jephthah and his daughter conclude must happen? (vv. 37-40)

This passage about the sacrifice of Jephthah's daughter has always disturbed me (as I am sure it does you). Some commentators think that God would not have expected Jephthah to fulfill his vow, but no where do we see God's intervention to prevent her sacrifice as He had done with Abraham and Isaac in Genesis 22:10-14. Others assert that the "sacrifice" was not his daughter's life, but that she would be doomed to perpetual virginity. As much as I would like to find an alternative ending to this terrible story that does not include the death of Jephthah's daughter, Scripture does not support that conclusion.

So let me go ahead and broach the question you are asking. Why would Jephthah make such a foolish vow?

Here are two possible reasons for Jephthah's vow:

- **Human sacrifice is how you pleased pagan gods.**
  In Jephthah's day, pagan cultures would offer a sacrifice to gain the favor of their gods. The greater the sacrifice, the greater favor you could earn from your god! Tim Keller observes that Jephthah is "infected…

by the pagan works-righteousness understanding of God's character."[13] God never condones this type of sacrifice. In fact, He condemns it. Deuteronomy 12:31 says, "You shall not behave thus toward the Lord your God, for every abominable act which the Lord hates they have done for their gods; for they even burn their sons and daughters in the fire to their gods."

- **Jephthah has become numb to the violence of his day.**

    The pagan moral code during the time of the Judges considered human life to be cheap when it came to military dominance. Jephthah allows the beliefs of the culture to infiltrate his true beliefs.

Jephthah reminds us of what happens when we fail to heed Paul's instruction in Romans 12:2, "And do not be conformed to this world, but be transformed by the renewing of your mind, so that you may prove what the will of God is, that which is good and acceptable and perfect." Modern day conforming to culture is what happens when a woman gets pregnant at an inconvenient time so she aborts the child (something that occurred 879,000 times in 2017 alone).[14] It is what occurs when a man decides that his marriage is no longer fulfilling so he leaves his wife and children for another woman (or a man).

Tomorrow, we will consider what we can learn from this terrible account in Israel's history. But as we close our study today, reflect on the culture around you. Is it influencing you? Your family? In what ways?

7. Read 2 Chronicles 7:14 and Habakkuk 3:2. As you reflect on the truths in these two verses, write a prayer of personal and/or corporate repentance.

WEEK 7 » DAY FOUR » JUDGES 11:39-12:7

As we saw yesterday, things just continue to deteriorate in Israel. Who would have thought that within 300 years of the Israelites entering the Promised Land, human sacrifice would be tolerated? On the other hand, in 1776, would any of the Founding Fathers who signed the Declaration of Independence proclaiming that life was an "unalienable right" ever have imagined that a law would be passed within two hundred years providing a woman the option to sacrifice a life for the sake of convenience?

A wise philosopher has said, "Those who cannot remember the past are condemned to repeat it."[15] A logical inference from that statement is that those who do not learn from the mistakes of the past are doomed to repeat them. Given that we all agree that Jephthah's sacrifice of his daughter was a heartbreaking tragedy, what lessons can we possibly learn from his mistakes?

First, **think before you speak**. Clearly, Jephthah did not think through the consequences of his words.

1. Read the following verses and write a one sentence summary for each of them.

    Psalm 141:3

    Proverbs 10:19

    Ephesians 4:29

    Colossians 4:6

    1 Peter 3:10

Second, **beware of the culturalization of your beliefs**. During the period of the Judges, the Israelites caved into the pagan cultures around them and were subsequently "Canaanized".

2. What are some ways to prevent culture from influencing you?

Third, **remember that God is a God of grace**. Had Jephthah confessed his rash vow to God, God clearly would have forgiven him. God is a forgiving, loving God of grace. As we read in 1 John 1:9, "If we confess our sins, He is faithful and righteous to forgive us our sins and to cleanse us from all unrighteousness."

3. Read Ephesians 1:5-8. What do you learn from this passage about God's thoughts toward you?

When the knowledge that God is for you, not against you, invades your heart, your life will be transformed.

I love the word "lavish" and the images it invokes. The fact that Paul uses this word to describe the grace of God toward us is a picture of an abundant, excessive, extravagant gift that we can do nothing to deserve yet He freely gives, should help us in our right view of God. God doesn't ration His grace. He lavishes us with it. Yet, the way we live is often a testimony to our struggle to believe that God is a God of grace. Write Ephesians 1:5-8 on an index card and meditate on it this week. As you do, you will see your mistrust and misunderstanding of God dissipate as your trust in His unconditional love for you increases. And when the knowledge that God is for you, not against you, invades your heart, your life will be transformed.

Lord,
I crawled across the barrenness to you
with my empty cup uncertain
in asking any small drop of refreshment.
If only I had known You better,
I'd have come running with a bucket.[16]
~Nancy Spiegelberg

If only Jephthah had understood the grace of God, his legacy would have been different. Instead, he dies with no heirs and his final chapter is a civil war in Israel.

Read Judges 12:1-7.

4. Summarize Ephraim's complaint. (v.1)

This sounds familiar doesn't it? In Judges 8:1-3, the men of Ephraim got upset with Gideon because they missed out on the glory of victory. Now jealous that Jephthah has been victorious over the Ammonites without their help, they cross the Jordan River and threaten to burn Jephthah's house down.

5. How does Jephthah respond? (vv.2-3)

The Ephraimites are not satisfied with Jephthah's answer and just like the Ammonites, they have come to Gilead armed for battle. When the Ephraimites speak insulting words about Jephthah's people, who were of the tribe of Manasseh, it is the final straw. Civil war breaks out between the Gileadites and the Ephraimites, and the Gileadites win. The Gileadites then seize the fords of the Jordan River, blocking the Ephraimites from crossing and returning to their home on the west side of the river. Once again, we see the importance of words.

6. What litmus test do the Gileadites devise to tell if someone trying to cross the Jordan River is an Ephraimite? (vv. 5-6)

Shibboleth is translated river, or an ear of corn in Hebrew. Easton's Bible Dictionary notes, "The tribes living on the east of Jordan, separated from their brethren on the west by the deep ravines and the rapid river, gradually came to adopt peculiar customs, and from mixing largely with the Moabites, Ishmaelites, and Ammonites to pronounce certain letters in such a manner as to distinguish them from the other tribes."[17]

7. How many Ephraimites are killed because of the way they pronounce *shibboleth*? (v. 6)

Jephthah serves as a judge in Israel only six years and then he dies. One commentary makes the following observation:

> The text merely notes the length of Jephthath's administration—six years—without reference to what has appeared in every story up to this point, except Abimelech's: they had peace. After Gideon (8:28), the land no longer enjoyed the Lord's gift of peace, even under the leadership of those He had raised up. The time of Jephthah, the subsequent minor judges (12:8-15), and Samson (chs. 13-16) was truly a transitional time for Israel, one from which there was no turning back. They had set their course to chaos by their resolute waywardness.[18]

As we see once again in Jephthah's story, God is continuing to be involved in the life of Israel. Even through their brokenness and faithlessness, He remains a Faithful KING.

8. Fill in the information on Jephthah on the chart on page 11.

Now, before we close the book on Jephthah, read Hebrews 11:32.

9. Given Jephthah's history, why do you think he is mentioned in the Hall of Faith?

God is able to take the mess of our past and turn it into a message.
He takes the trials and tests and turns them into a testimony.[19]
~Christine Caine

WEEK 7 » DAY FIVE » JUDGES 12:8-15

When our oldest son was pre-school age, he loved to pretend that he was Superman. He would grab his red cape and "fly" throughout the house pretending that he was "faster than a speeding bullet, more powerful than a locomotive, and able to leap tall buildings at a single bound." There was something about the secret identity of mild-mannered reporter, Clark Kent, that seized his imagination and allowed him to envision himself also being able to achieve heroic actions.

Just what is it that makes Superman so appealing, not only to children, but to all of us? Is it his power to change the course of mighty rivers and bend steel with his bare hands? Is it his unwavering duty to fight a never-ending battle for Truth, Justice, and the American Way? Or is it something else?

As you remember, Superman, despite his super-powers had a vulnerable spot. When he came in contact with Kryptonite, the only mineral that survived the annihilation of his childhood planet, he would be weakened to the point of losing all of his powers. Metaphorically, Kryptonite is synonymous with weakness. Brokenness. To put it in a biblical framework, sin.

All of Israel's judges are flawed individuals by virtue of their own humanity. In many cases, their flaws are detailed as much, if not more than, their leadership. As we encounter their weaknesses, brokenness, and besetting sins, we wonder what more they could have accomplished…if only they had dealt with their own form of Kryptonite. And as we wonder, we find a seed of hope as we see who and what God uses to accomplish His purposes. A left-handed man with a homemade sword. A woman with a tent peg. A farmer with a fear problem. A local reject with a past.

God saves the unworthy and qualifies the unqualified not because of the greatness of their deeds, but because of the greatness of His grace through Jesus Christ, the One True Deliverer, on our behalf. And when He calls us to His purpose for our lives, He expects us to move forward, dealing with our weakness, brokenness, and sin as we go, so that He can demonstrate His supernatural power in and through us.

We'll come back to that. But first, let's meet the next three judges in Israel.

Read Judges 12:8-15.

There are not a lot of standout details given about these three judges. They were simply ordinary men that God called to be leaders during their time on God's history line. Three regular people who were available to God and used by God.

1. Go back and read Judges 10:6 and then turn the page forward and read Judges 13:1. How do these verses describe the state of the Israelites before the judgeship of Jephthah and then after Ibzan, Elon, and Abdon served as judges?

2. What is the combined total of years that Ibzan, Elon, and Abdon judged Israel? (vv. 8-15)

During all of this time, there is no mention of God's people wandering away from Him and "doing evil" or having to suffer at the hands of their enemies. Apparently, these three men protected the peace and kept order in the land.

3. After Jephthah dies, Ibzan becomes the next judge of Israel. There is a stark contrast between Jephthah and Ibzan. What is it?

It is possible that some of the matchmaking that is mentioned in Ibzan's brief story was done to build alliances and make peace with the tribes surrounding Bethlehem. It is interesting to note that there were two Bethlehem's during this time. One was in Judah, the town where Jesus was born. The other was in Zebulon, about ten miles north of Megiddo.[20] Although no one is totally sure, many believe that Ibzan lived in the latter area.

Although we are given little information about Ibzan, we read even less biographical information about Elon.

4. By what name is Elon called? (vv.11-12)

The tribe of Zebulun lived in the area to the north of Issachar and south of Asher and Naphtali (Joshua 19:10-16), and between the Sea of Galilee and the Mediterranean Sea (see map on page 7). This part of Galilee was where a large part of Jesus' ministry took place.[21]

Elon is honored to be a member of the tribe of Zebulun and he makes sure that the people he is leading know it.

5. How do our words about our city and our country impact us and influence others?

In verse 13, we read that Abdon, the son of Hillel, and a citizen of Pirathon, becomes the next judge of Israel (v. 13). Pirathon was a city in Ephraim (see map on page 7) which means that Abdon is a member of the tribe that had suffered great losses two decades before when they attempted to attack Jephthah and the Gileadites (see 12:1-7). Abdon's judgeship is a testimony of his ability to lead his people to restoration.

Now granted, riding on donkeys probably doesn't impress you or interest you. But in Abdon's day, having donkey transportation was like having a fleet of limousines at your disposal. (Remember the words in Deborah's Song about donkeys (5:10) and Jair's story in 10:3-5.) This symbol of nobility and power gives us insight into Abdon's accomplishments.

6. Fill in the chart on page 11 with information on Ibzan, Elon, and Abdon, three men who served their people well and maintained peace.

My phone just rang. Literally. The voice on the other end of the phone delivered the news that someone I know, someone several years younger than me, died during the night. My first thought when I heard the news? A life wasted. Not because of his death, but because of his life. He was a person that God created with a divine purpose, a purpose that if fulfilled would bring glory to Him. Sadly, this person chose rebellion over obedience, self over the Savior. And in the end, his Kryptonite reduced him to nothing.

Have you ever known someone who wasted his or her life? A person created in the image of God with the potential to do great things but he or she just threw it all away?

Week 7 | 159

Repeatedly, our study in Judges demonstrates the tragic end of replicating sin cycles in our lives. But it also shows us how God can use an ordinary person to do extraordinary things, if that person yields their life completely to Him. As John Piper writes, "God created me–and you–to live with a single, all-embracing, all-transforming passion–namely, a passion to glorify God by enjoying and displaying His supreme excellence in all the spheres of life."[22]

How is God speaking to you? Do you need to put an end to a sin cycle in your life? Or do you just need to step out in faith and walk in purposeful obedience to God? Spend some time in prayer right now, talking with God about what He shows you.

Remember, this is YOUR time on the history line of God. Get up on your feet and get after it! No excuses. No delays. No red cape needed. In the words of the writer of Hebrews,

> Strip down, start running–and never quit! No extra spiritual fat, no parasitic sins. Keep your eyes on *Jesus*, who both began and finished this race we're in. Study how he did it. Because he never lost sight of where he was headed–that exhilarating finish in and with God–he could put up with anything along the way: Cross, shame, whatever. And now he's *there*, in the place of honor, right alongside God. When you find yourselves flagging in your faith, go over that story again, item by item, that long litany of hostility he plowed through. *That* will shoot adrenaline into your souls! (Hebrews 12:1-2, MSG)

7. Reflect on the ways God has spoken to you this week. Be specific.

But whatever you do, find the God-centered, Christ-exalting, Bible-saturated passion of your life, and find your way to say it and live for it and die for it. And you will make a difference that lasts. You will not waste your life.[23]
~John Piper

When the Weak Becomes Strong
Judges 13-14

God is at work for and through His flawed people.[1]
~Tim Keller

Potential and incredible opportunity. This is what lay at the feet of Samson. He is born with credentials like no other and is truly to be "set apart to God from the womb" (Judges 13:5, BSB). The repetitive rebellion on the part of the Israelites sets the stage for Philistine oppression. God marks Samson before he is even born, desiring to use him to bring deliverance to His people once again. God will use Samson (a flawed person) to set a path of deliverance for the Israelites (a flawed people). Through this, we will see again the faithfulness of our King.

Our call may not be that of Samson's, but as a child of God, we have been marked and called out for a purpose…one that is specific to us. As we begin our study of Samson, I pray we will walk away with a determination to fulfill God's call on our lives…starting *and* finishing strong.

WEEK 8 » DAY ONE » JUDGES 13:1

Read Judges 13:1.

1. What difference do you see in this verse as compared with earlier chapters we have studied? What element is missing?

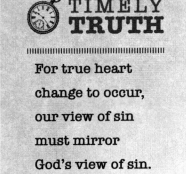

For true heart change to occur, our view of sin must mirror God's view of sin.

We have read many times in previous chapters that the Israelites cried out to the Lord. While this was more of a cry for relief than a cry of repentance, they did cry out for help. Their cry is missing from Judges 13. This would lead us to believe that they have grown complacent and are accustomed to oppression.

One should find this reality both troubling and heartbreaking. How can a people who had been powerfully delivered from multiple enemies find themselves content with servitude? For true heart change to occur, our view of sin must mirror God's view of sin.

Judges 13 opens this way, "Again the Israelites did evil **in the eyes of the LORD**…" (Judges 13:1, NIV, emphasis mine). Perhaps the seemingly never-ending sin cycle is due to the Israelites' view, or lack thereof, of their sin. Tim Keller says, "This term 'the eyes of the LORD,' in contrast with our 'own eyes,' teaches us that sin does not ultimately consist of violating our conscience or violating our personal standards or violating community standards, but rather consists of violating God's will for us."[2]

Our society functions with a mindset that says, "What's good for you is good for you. What's true for me is true for me." This mentality flies in the face of the Word of God.

2. Read John 17:17. How should we derive our truth?

As we see the Israelites repeatedly falling into a cycle of sin and now reaching the point of not even asking the Lord for relief, we easily recognize their view of sin is not in line with the law they were once given.

Sin is deceptive. At the heart of the Israelites' sin is idolatry. Truth be told, the same goes for us. We choose disobedience because something else has taken God's rightful place in our hearts. Something has replaced Him as the Supreme Authority.

3. Think of a sin you've recently committed. How quickly were you convicted? How did you respond?

Was your heart broken for what breaks God's heart? Did you find yourself longing to be made right with your Heavenly Father? Or were you casual about it? Did you justify it in your mind or consider it a "small" sin? We can learn a valuable lesson from Judges 13. Samson is the last of the judges in the book of Judges, however, we have yet to see a genuine, lasting heart change in the people of Israel.

4. What are common sins we often categorize as "small" or not so grievous in "our eyes?"

5. Pause and ask the Spirit of God to shine a holy spotlight onto your heart. Are there "small" sins you have minimized for which you need to confess and repent?

In closing, ponder Tim Keller's thoughts on this topic.

> This should lead us to be very careful constantly to evaluate ourselves, through reflection on the Bible and through personal accountability to others. We are always finding ways to rationalize sins such as materialism or worry or bitterness or pride. They don't look bad in "our eyes." As the seventeenth-century Puritan writer, Thomas Brooks, put it: "Satan paints sin with virtue's colors."[3]

Before we begin observing the beginning of Samson's life and God's call for him, we will benefit greatly to have enlightened spiritual eyes, clearly seeing God's view of sin and committing to align ourselves with it.

Open the eyes of my heart, Lord.

> *...asking God, the glorious Father of our Lord Jesus Christ, to give you spiritual wisdom and insight so that you might grow in your knowledge of God.*
> ~Ephesians 1:17, NLT

WEEK 8 » DAY TWO » JUDGES 13:1-5

Let us begin today's study by adding to our chart as well as finding our place on the sin cycle.

Read Judges 13:1-2.

1. What stages of the sin cycle do we find in these verses? Make a note on the diagram below for the opening verses of Judges 13.

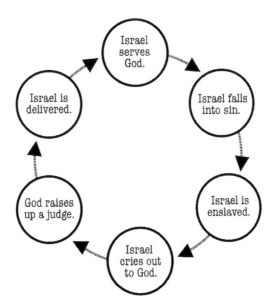

As we've seen throughout this study (and throughout the Bible for that matter), God's attributes of mercy and grace shine brightly once again. While the Israelites do not cry out for help, the Lord steps in and offers a gracious rescuer. Dale Ralph Davis says, "For if Yahweh's help were given only when we prayed for it, only when we asked for it, only when we had sense enough to seek it, what paupers and orphans we would be."[4]

2. To whom does the Lord hand over the Israelites and for how long (v. 1)? (Use this information to fill in *The Judges of Israel* chart on page 11.)

Quickly, the details begin to unfold.

3. Who are Samson's parents and from which tribe did they come (v. 2)? (Add to your chart on page 11.)

4. What facts are given about Samson's mother?

These details are noteworthy. Not only is Samson's mother barren, which carried a cultural stigma of an insecure and insignificant future, but she is also unnamed. Barren *and* obscure. Wouldn't you assume these realities would leave her feeling hopeless?

Again, the Lord plans to bring salvation out of seemingly hopeless circumstances. This is the gospel of Jesus Christ. No matter who you are, no matter the circumstances you've endured, no matter the mistakes you've made, there is hope! There is hope because of a Savior!

We see the Lord unfolding His plan. The angel of the Lord appears to Manoah's wife and gives her instructions for rearing the baby in her womb. These commands are from the Nazirite vow we find in Numbers 6:1-21. The word *Nazirite* comes from a Hebrew word that means "to separate, to consecrate."[5]

5. What are the specifics given to her in verses 3-5?

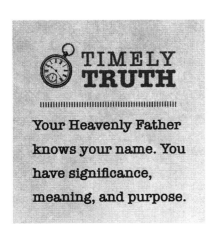

TIMELY TRUTH

Your Heavenly Father knows your name. You have significance, meaning, and purpose.

I want us to spend some time focusing on God offering hope through hopelessness and the importance of an obedient and committed heart.

Many commentaries note the significance of Samson's birth and how it points to THE Savior. God births Samson for the purpose of deliverance. God sends Jesus as the ultimate Deliverer. God brings Samson to an unnamed woman who has suffered the shame of barrenness among her people. God gives us Jesus through a young, virgin girl who would suffer ridicule and shame due to an unexplainable pregnancy.

Week 8 | 166

Oh, how I pray you see and are reminded how our God moves and works. Like Samson's mother, you may not be known in this world, but you are known in the kingdom of God. Your Heavenly Father knows your name. You have significance, meaning, and purpose.

Isaiah 49:16 (NLT) tells us, "See, I have written your name on the palms of my hands."

6. Read Isaiah 55:8-11 and as you do, reflect on Samson's mother. How do these verses speak to your heart?

As you walk through dark times in this life, as you encounter broken people (or find yourself broken), be reminded of our Faithful King. He put you together. He knows your name. He has a specific plan and purpose for your life. This sinful world and the devil himself will bombard you with thoughts of doubt. If you fall prey to these lies, you may miss out on God's perfect plan.

God's plan is to raise up another mighty warrior in Samson, and He uses the least of these to bring him into the world.

7. How have you seen God bring hope out of hopelessness in your life? Consider sharing with your small group.

Then you will know that I am the LORD; those who hope in Me will not be disappointed.
~Isaiah 49:23b (NIV)

WEEK 8 » DAY THREE » JUDGES 13:6-25

There is a mystery, a depth, a surpassingness about God that we can never fathom, comprehend or touch.[6]
~Dale Ralph Davis

Today, we will see the faith and obedience of Samson's parents in response to the visits from the angel of the Lord. This passage of Scripture is packed full of rich truths and powerful applications.

Read Judges 13:6-25.

1. How is the faith of Samson's parents revealed in verses 6-8?

Samson's mother believes the Lord can do the impossible. She has a similar response as Mary in Luke 1:38, "May it be done to me according to your Word." She also walks in obedience to the Lord's command to keep the Nazirite vow for both herself (as it would affect her unborn baby) and for Samson.

Manoah's response in prayer shows faith on his part as well. He longs to walk in obedience to the Lord by making sure to follow His command completely.

2. What does Manoah pray in verse 8? Why?

The Lord graciously sends the angel back in response to Manoah's prayer, but he does not offer new information. The angel simply reminds him that his wife is to follow the instructions previously given. Manoah asks the angel to stay so he can prepare a burnt offering as a sacrifice to the Lord. "With the grain offering, Manoah showed his desire to serve God and demonstrated his respect."[7]

As God often does, He gives more to Manoah than he requested. Manoah wants the angel to repeat and possibly elaborate on the rules given to his wife. The angel has something better than a list of rules.

Tim Keller explains it this way. "Manoah prayed for help, and that help was apparently refused. But in fact, Manoah *did* get the help he needed, but not in the *form* he was asking for. He wanted to know 'what is to be the *rule* for the boy's life and work?' (v. 12) – to have more regulations. Instead, God gives Manoah a revelation of who He is."[8]

3. What does Manoah ask in verse 17?

4. How does the angel respond in verse 18?

I love this! If you could just see me typing right now! I am sitting up on my knees in my chair, fingers going as fast as they can, a smile spread wide across my face and a heart that is overflowing.

God, in His character, is far beyond our wildest dreams. While many of us know Him intimately and experience Him in ways we cannot explain, there is even more. His name is beyond understanding, too wonderful for us to comprehend. In this statement, I imagine God saying to Manoah (and to us), "I want you to know **Me**."

God's laws and instructions are vastly important. They are meant to be followed and obeyed without compromise. But even more than knowing the words of His Word (information), He wants us to know HIM.

5. Read verses 19 and 20. What does God do here?

If we are watching (v. 19), God will do amazing things. "As the flames from the altar shot up toward the sky, the angel of the LORD ascended in the fire" (Judges 13:20a, NLT). Tim Keller says, "He indelibly prints in their minds His greatness."[9]

In dark times and among broken people, our Faithful King will display His greatness.

6. How are you watching with anticipation and expectation?

7. What reactions do you see from Samson's parents in verses 21-23?

Fear and joy. Manoah fears the Lord (based on Exodus 33:20). Samson's mother rejoices in that which she confidently believes. The Lord desires both of these in our lives. Fear of the Lord is absolutely necessary in the heart of a believer who longs to walk closely with the Lord and experience His blessing and revelation. Joy in the Lord, as a result of a faith-filled life, is required for strength as we journey through this life. "We need a properly balanced response to the presence of God."[10]

Bible study is important to and imperative in the life of a believer. We cannot expect revelation and blessing if we do not regularly digest the truth of God's Word. However, if we are not careful, we can view this time as a checklist or a time to simply gain more head knowledge. As we take in the Bread of Life through the Word of God and practice the disciplines of Bible reading and prayer, we will experience the presence of God. We may not see with our physical eyes the same as Manoah and his wife, but oh dear sister, we can surely see Him with spiritual eyes. As they saw flames shoot up from the altar, the fire of the Holy Spirit can penetrate our hearts and leave us burning with a passionate desire to know Him more.

Honestly evaluate your relationship with Jesus Christ as you read through these questions. Consider making notes as you go, using this as a time of confession and praise.

- As you meet with Him each day, do you approach Him with both fear and joy?

- Does your heart burn as you open the Bible and read God's Words to you?

- When you bow in prayer, do you sense His presence and find yourself in awe that He is with you?

- As you go about your day, do you see His hand, acknowledging His care for the details of your life?

- Do you genuinely want more of Him?

Can you say, as Brother Lawrence, "When I am with Him there, nothing frightens me, but the slightest diversion away from Him is painful to me"?[11]

Commit today to know the Father deeply, intimately, personally. While we cannot fully know Him this side of Heaven, we can spend our days pressing in closely to hear the heartbeat of our Savior. The deepest satisfaction and greatest joy you've known pales in comparison to knowing Him.

May your soul's appetite be satisfied at the Lord's table.

WEEK 8 » DAY FOUR » JUDGES 13

Before we continue on to our study of Judges 14, I want us to pause and contemplate the presence of God. Over the course of the last 24 hours, the Lord has pressed upon my heart the importance of this. Brother Lawrence has well said, "I still believe that all spiritual life consists of practicing God's presence and that anyone who practices it correctly will soon attain spiritual fulfillment. There is no sweeter manner of living in the world than continuous communion with God."[12]

I cannot help but think how differently life might have played out for the children of Israel if they had been solely focused on the presence of God. God's purpose was ultimately fulfilled, even through the sinful choices of His people; however, as you and I walk through this study, I pray we will make every effort to avoid missing His perfect plan. I believe we can do this by practicing the presence of God, keeping our eyes fixed on Him. This will help us from falling into a similar pattern of repeating the sin cycle of the Israelites.

Consider Samson. If he'd been faithfully and intentionally seeking the presence of the Lord rather than doing what was right in his own eyes (as the Israelites did), he may have suffered less throughout the account of Judges. While God, in His sovereignty, empowers him to be victorious on several occasions, Samson's life is not marked by surrender and obedience.

Pastor Rick Warren shares this:

> The classic book on learning how to develop a constant conversation with God is *Practicing the Presence of God*, written in the 17th century by Brother Lawrence, a humble cook in a French monastery. Brother Lawrence was able to turn even the most commonplace and menial tasks—like preparing meals and washing dishes—into acts of praise and communion with God. The key to friendship with God, he said, is not changing what you do, but changing *your attitude* toward what you do. What you normally do for yourself, you begin doing for God, whether it is eating, bathing, working, relaxing, or taking out the trash.[13]

Like all disciplines, whether physical or spiritual, living continuously in the presence of God takes practice. We must set our minds to do it…until we just do it. It can become a way of life for us. This is God's desire for you and me. If we choose to practice the presence of God, we minimize our opportunities to fall back into those old sinful patterns. Unfortunately, we will not be completely without sin until we enter Heaven, but we can refuse to spin endlessly on the sin cycle wheel.

1. Record the benefits of being in God's presence.

    Psalm 16:11

    James 4:8

    Psalm 46:10

    Exodus 33:16

2. What are some things that keep us from God's presence?

    Ephesians 4:30a

    1 Thessalonians 5:19-22

    Exodus 32:7-8

3. How do you enter into the presence of God, even in the midst of your mundane tasks? What stands in your way of doing so?

Oh, how He longs to be with you. The Creator of the universe desires to be with <u>you</u>. Make this Psalm a prayer today. If you are unable to honestly declare it, pray it each day until the Lord makes it the authentic cry of your heart.

> *O God, you are my God;*
>
> *I earnestly search for you.*
>
> *My soul thirsts for you;*
>
> *My whole body longs for you*
>
> *In this parched and weary land*
>
> *Where there is no water.*
>
> *I have seen you in your sanctuary*
>
> *And gazed upon your power and glory.*
>
> *Your unfailing love is better than life itself;*
>
> *How I praise you!*
>
> *I will praise you as long as I live,*
>
> *Lifting up my hands to you in prayer.*
>
> *You satisfy me more than the richest feast.*
>
> *I will praise you with songs of joy.*
>
> *I lie awake thinking of you,*
>
> *Meditating on you through the night.*
>
> *Because you are my helper,*
>
> *I sing for joy in the shadow of your wings.*
>
> *I cling to you;*
>
> *Your strong right hand holds me securely.*
>
> *(Psalm 63:1-8, NLT)*

Had Samson chosen to follow his parents' example of responding to the Lord's presence with reverent fear and joy, he may have avoided the pitfalls of being impulsive and unteachable. Choosing to enter in and remain in the presence of God is life changing. We will not live a life free of sin and pain, but we can powerfully stand in dark times and among broken people if we practice the presence of our Faithful King!

When you are discouraged, His presence will see you through. When you are lonely, His presence will cheer you up. When you are worried, His presence will calm you down. When you are tempted, His presence will help you out. [14]
~Dr. Adrian Rogers

WEEK 8 » DAY FIVE » JUDGES 14:1-20

Today, we begin to see why many call Samson the most flawed character in the book of Judges.

This is said of him at the close of chapter 13, "and the Spirit of the LORD began to stir him…" (Judges 13:25a). Samson is a grown man by the end of chapter 13 and is being stirred by the Spirit of the Lord. How does he quickly derail to a life impacted by his own impulses rather than the influence of the Spirit? (Consider our study yesterday as you work through today.)

1. Read Judges 14:1-3. What do Samson's words reveal about his heart?

Warren Wiersbe says, "Samson was a man of faith, but he certainly wasn't a faithful man."[15] Samson's parents raise him to honor the Lord by following His laws, which include the Nazirite vow. Nevertheless, he wanders into enemy territory and is captivated by a foreign woman.

2. Read Deuteronomy 7:1-4. Why is Samson's decision to marry a Philistine woman wrong?

3. Reread Judges 14:3. What word does Samson's father use to describe the Philistines?

I love Tim Keller's commentary on this point:

> Circumcision was a sign that a family was in a personal covenant or relationship with God, as part of His people. Their issue was not a racial one. It is about marriage with someone outside of the Lord's covenant. God's prohibition (Exodus 34:15-16) is not again inter-racial marriage, but against inter-faith marriage (for instance, Moses was married to a non-Israelite, Zipporah, but one who recognized God's covenant; see Exodus 4:24-26).[16]

Our God sees and values the heart. As the Lord said to Samuel when he was searching to anoint a king, "Don't judge by his appearance or height, for I have rejected him. The LORD doesn't see things the way you see them. People judge by outward appearance, but the LORD looks at the heart" (1 Samuel 16:7, NLT).

4. Read 1 John 2:16. How does this verse speak to what's taking place in Samson's life?

5. How do you see the sin cycle of the Israelites reflected in Samson's response to his father in verse 3?

The text goes on to reveal an interesting, and sometimes confusing, characteristic of God.

6. Read Judges 14:4. What does this verse tell us of God and His purpose?

Dale Ralph Davis explains it this way, "It means that neither Samson's foolishness nor his stubbornness is going to prevent Yahweh from accomplishing His design. Yahweh can and will use the sinfulness or stupidity of his servants as the camouflage for bringing His secret will to pass."[17]

Isn't it hard to imagine, within the confines of our human mind, that Almighty God would accomplish His purpose in the midst of our sin? Warren Wiersbe says, "When God isn't permitted to rule in our lives, He overrules and works out His will in spite of our decisions. Of course, we're the losers for rebelling against Him, but God will accomplish His purposes either with us or in spite of us."[18]

Other great examples of this are the Old Testament accounts of Daniel, Esther, and Joseph. God takes the sinful actions of man and uses them for the good of His children and for His glory.

7. What does Genesis 50:20 tell us about God's purposes?

We see the most powerful example of this in the death of Jesus Christ. The acts of sinful men led to the crucifixion of Jesus Christ, which God used to offer us redemption from sin and the gift of eternal life! (See Acts 2:23-24.)

8. Read Judges 14:5-9. What does Samson do to further disobey God?

As Samson veers off the main road and away from his parents, he ends up in a vineyard (not a good place for someone who was to abstain from alcoholic drink) and is attacked by a lion. Again, we see the Holy Spirit empowering him to defeat the enemy (using evil for good), but he continues to disobey as he pursues a marriage that dishonors the Lord. He further defiles his body by eating honey from the carcass of the lion and then offering it to his parents without telling them from where it had come.

It is important to see the gradual decline of Samson's life as he makes one poor decision after another. Dear child of God, you must be ever alert to the instructions of the Lord and the tactics of the enemy to pull you off the path that leads to life. The devil "prowls around like a roaring lion, seeking someone to devour" (1 Peter 5:8, ESV). Just like the Holy Spirit empowered Samson to defeat the lion, He has given you strength to defeat the enemy. Unlike Samson, I encourage you to experience His power as you stay the course of faithful obedience.

The remainder of chapter 14 goes on to show Samson's lack of control with his tongue and his temper.

9. Briefly describe the events of verses 10 through 18.

Warren Wiersbe says this of Samson's riddle, "Sad to say, he constructed the riddle out of the experience of his sin! He didn't take seriously the fact that he had violated his Nazirite vows. It's bad enough to disobey God, but when you make a joke out of it, you've sunk to new depths of spiritual insensitivity."[19]

It is important to note the danger in this. We live in a society where talk is cheap and sin is taken lightly, even among Christians. We must be careful as we choose our words. Are they true? Do they honor the Lord Jesus Christ and point others to Him? Samson's words not only displayed his disregard for his sin, but he also set a plan into motion that would place his wife and her family in danger (v. 16). Our sin affects the lives of those closest to us.

Judges 14 closes with Samson's display of anger (vv. 19-20). While the Spirit of the Lord gives him strength, he uses it impulsively to kill thirty men from Ashkelon and take their belongings so he can satisfy the bet he has lost. He is so furious about what has taken place that he goes back to his parents' house before even consummating his marriage. Verse 20 tells us, "So his wife was given in marriage to the man who had been Samson's best man at the wedding" (NLT).

So what originally led to Samson's disobedience (his desire to marry a Philistine woman) does not even come to fruition. Here again, we see God stepping in, even in the midst of Samson's sin, to begin the deliverance of Israel from the Philistines. Remember that God promises that Samson would *begin* to save Israel from the Philistines (13:5). Here we see the beginning of it.

I'll close this week's study with a page from my youngest son's quote book from this past school year. He showed me this page on the morning I planned to write this last day. What a beautiful reminder that our Faithful King is the Master Weaver.

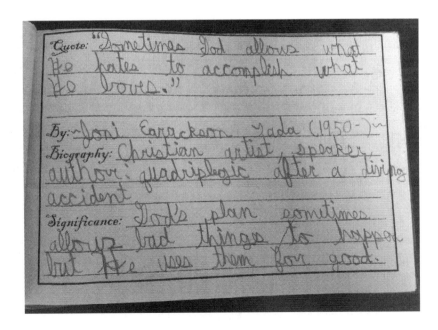

When the Strong Becomes Weak
Judges 15-16

One of the most important parts of digging into Old Testament stories is our inevitable encounter with the depths of sin and its effects on the human race.[1]
~ Kathleen Nielson

As we have been working through the book of Judges, we have seen that the judges themselves grow increasingly weak as the years of oppression grow increasingly longer. Oh how patient God is in the midst of His children's rebellion! How often we think we know better than God and that we can create a comfortable existence apart from Him and His design.

Trying to build a life outside of God's will and design always leads to oppression and heartache. It may not be the oppression of a foreign nation, but it will always lead to oppression and bondage. We can see in our own country the oppression of drug addiction, immorality, poverty, and the brokenness of the family.

In Judges 15 we continue the narrative of Samson. This man, chosen before he was born to lead God's people and free them from the Philistines, has been reckless and driven by lust. As a quick review, let's recall what has happened thus far. This man who was to free his people from the Philistines, decides he wants to marry one of the daughters of the Philistines. He is careless with his commitment to his Nazaritic vow as he touches a dead animal when he eats the honey in the body of the lion. In Judges 14:10, the feast mentioned is one that would have included alcohol, violating his vow.

Samson challenges the Philistine young men gathered for the wedding festivities with a riddle and promises them thirty garments of clothes if they can figure it out. The men put pressure on the young woman he is betrothed to and threaten to burn her family if she doesn't find out the answer to the riddle. She weeps and presses Samson to tell her, which he does on the last day of the feast. The Philistine men have the answer just in time. Samson becomes so angry that he strikes down thirty men, taking their clothes in payment and in "hot anger" goes back to his father's house (Judges 14:19).

Even if you have never heard or read about Samson, you can already tell that this impulsive and hotheaded young man is intent on getting what he wants. He is a man of unbridled passion and he believes God will keep blessing him even though he is not obeying His Word or honoring his vow as a Nazarite.

WEEK 9 » DAY ONE » JUDGES 15:1-8

When Samson returns to Timnah, he has cooled off. His plan is to reconcile with his wife and consummate their marriage. He hopes his "heifer" (14:18) will be eager to welcome him, but just in case, he brings her a present. A goat. Not flowers or candy. A goat. This guy really has a lot to learn in the romance department.

Read Judges 15:1-8.

1. What surprising news does Samson find out when he arrives at his wife's house? (v. 2)

Although his wife's father offers her younger, more attractive sister to Samson, he is in no mood for a wife upgrade. He is seething with anger, and he intends to make the Philistines pay for it.

2. Describe Samson's revenge. (vv. 4-5)

Remember that this happens during the time of the wheat harvest. The wheat is harvested, but is not threshed. Shocks of wheat were standing upright in the fields. When he sets the foxes loose in the middle of the crops, the fire quickly spreads, destroying not only the wheat crop, but also the vineyards and the olive groves. The Philistines are an agricultural people and Samson has just struck a devastating blow to their economy.

3. When the Philistines find out that Samson was taking vengeance on the Philistines because his wife was given by her father to the best man, how do they retaliate? (vv. 6-8)

The vengeance of the Philistines serves only to escalate matters. Samson now feels justified to attack and slaughter a number of Philistines. Tim Keller notes, "The violence is ratcheting up, retaliation after retaliation. Without forgiveness and reconciliation, it is a familiar story to us, both within family structures and on national levels."[2]

Have you ever been tempted to seek revenge?

4. Describe a time when you desired or sought revenge.

5. We quite often believe that God will only work through people who have the right beliefs and behavior. How do we know this is not true?

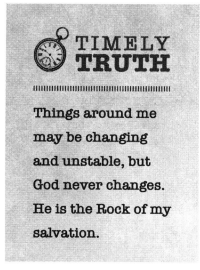

Things around me may be changing and unstable, but God never changes. He is the Rock of my salvation.

Samson is acting like a toddler. My grandchildren often have meltdowns when they don't get what they want or another child thwarts their plan by taking their toy or taking over what they were doing. If I am quite honest, I see myself in them at times. How often do I think I know how God should answer my prayer? Or I think I know how He should work in a relationship, or this person's life, and yet He doesn't work on my timetable or according to my ideas.

How will I respond? Will I trust the Lord and know that He is good and only does good? Circumstances and the schemes of the enemy do not change the fact that my Father is good. Things around me may be changing and unstable, but God never changes. He is the Rock of my salvation. He is the stronghold into which I run when all around me is shaking (Proverbs 18:10).

6. How would things be different for you if you turned to Christ instead of someone else or even to revenge?

WEEK 9 » DAY TWO » JUDGES 15:9-20

The Philistines realize that their best course of action is a search and destroy mission with Samson as their target.

Read Judges 15:9-20.

1. Which tribe do the Philistines approach about helping them capture Samson?

How could the very tribe that was the first to possess their inheritance not recognize God's deliverance and instead work for their oppressors?

2. Why do you think they have become so comfortable in oppression?

Tim Keller gives insight into the spiritual condition of Judah:

> Judah is so keen to remain at peace with them that they have no idea that God has raised up a judge to save Israel (v. 10)! And when they discover that he has, they send 3,000 men to hand the judge over to their enemy (v. 11-12)! They may bear the name of God's people, but they would rather live at peace with the world and worship their idols than be freed to worship God – and they would rather cut down their own rescuer than risk confrontation with the world.[3]

3. Read Judges 15:14. What does it say came upon Samson?

4. Where else have we seen these words: "the Spirit of the Lord came upon him" pertaining to Samson?

This will be the last time we see these words in relation to Samson. What a sad statement. But so it is with many of us. Have you ever known someone who was extremely gifted and yet lacked spiritual depth and holiness? God had given his people His promises of blessing if they would obey His Word. These same promises pertain to us today. God has not changed; He is the same yesterday, today and forever (Hebrews 13:8).

5. Read Deuteronomy 28:1-14 and underline the blessings God desires for His people.

6. Read Deuteronomy 28:15-20 and underline the curses. The rest of the chapter foretells what will happen to God's people when they rebel and refuse to repent. What a sad commentary on the state of the hearts of humanity!

7. Moses reviews the words of the covenant with the people in Deuteronomy 28-30 and calls on them to choose life. Write out the words of Deuteronomy 30:19.

You might also want to put them on a 3x5 card and put it in a prominent place. Day by day, moment by moment, we must CHOOSE life. We know the truth and we must CHOOSE Him!

How is it that we who have the full revelation of God's Word and the cross can still so often resort to our own reasoning and live as we see fit, believing God will still bless us? Just because God is patient and long-suffering does not negate His holiness or His faithfulness to His Word. We will be judged for our actions in the flesh (2 Corinthians 5:10).

8. What weaknesses are evident in the life of Samson? Make a list from Judges 15.

WEEK 9 » DAY THREE » JUDGES 16:1-21

Samson has now personally killed over 1,000 Philistines, but has failed to lead Israel to take any steps toward obedience. And he just assumes that God will continue to bless him regardless of how many times he gives in to his weakness.

Read Judges 16:1-3.

When Samson goes to Gaza, he is venturing deep into Philistine territory. Gaza is a very ancient city, situated close to the Mediterranean Sea in the southern part of Philistine territory. Although we don't know why Samson heads to Gaza, it is unlikely that his primary reason is to find sensual pleasure. There are plenty of prostitutes in Israel even though the law forbids this practice (Leviticus 19:29).

1. However, what happens when Samson arrives in Gaza?

2. What does this tell you about Samson and his lust?

3. How does Samson escape and why do you think he chooses to do this?

One theologian notes:

> The incident of Samson removing the doors of Gaza showed that his physical strength was unmatched except by his moral weakness. No reason is given why Samson went to Gaza, perhaps the most important Philistine city, which was near the coast about 35 miles southwest of his home in Zorah. Whatever the reason, his sensual inclination overcame him and he spent the night with a prostitute.[4]

Read Judges 16:4-21.

For the third time Samson becomes infatuated with a woman from Philistia, Delilah, from the Valley of Sorek. Samson will use Delilah to meet his needs and Delilah will use him to fulfill her greed. They were both using each other. Have you ever felt used or have you ever used someone for your own personal gain?

Apparently Samson's weakness for women is well known by the Philistines. They have also learned their lesson and know not to engage Samson in his full strength. So they decide to use his weakness for Delilah for their benefit:

> Once the Philistine authorities learned of the attachment of Samson to Delilah, they formulated their plans. These included the formal visit of the five lords of the Philistine cities of Gaza, Ashkelon, Ashdod, Gath, and Ekron to Delilah and the divulgence of international intrigue. So completely did they trust her and her ability to do the job that each of the lords offered 1,100 pieces of silver, 5,500 in all![5]

Delilah presses Samson just as the woman he had been betrothed to had pressed him. His weak character is unable to withstand the pressure and he gives in again.

4. Why do you think he gives in?

5. Samson has depended upon the gift of his strength instead of depending upon God. What gifts has God given you and do you ever depend upon His gift or natural abilities instead of upon God?

I read a poem once that pertains to the foolishness of doing the same thing over and over and yet expecting different results. I wrote about it in *Choose Wisely, Live Fully*: "The title of the poem was, 'Autobiography in Five Short Chapters.' In chapter one, which is verse one, a person walks down a street and falls into a deep hole. The person moves from pretending not to see the hole to trying to avoid the hole only to find themselves back at the bottom every time.

Unfortunately, it takes the person to the fifth chapter to finally decide to walk down another street."[6]

Why do we find ourselves dealing with the same sin over and over and over? Could it be that we think we have learned our lesson and surely will not fall for the same thing again only to walk too close to the hole one more time? Then we are shocked when we find ourselves right back where we started. The only way to change the result is to change the path. We must change what we are doing before we will change the outcome!

The only way to change our actions is to change our thinking. The enemy is constantly hurling fiery darts of discouragement, fear and hopelessness at us. When we are focused on ourselves, we are more likely to give in to temptation. That is why it is imperative that we practice taking our thoughts captive (2 Corinthians 10:3-5) and replacing lies with truth. But to be able to do this, we must know the truth! Knowing the truth is how we discern the lie. Then we must refuse the lie and instead think on what is true. The truth is life to our souls.

I read an article recently about a Freedom March in Washington, DC. This march was planned and promoted by men and women who had come to Christ and been set free from homosexuality and transgenderism. One of the people interviewed, Angel Colon, survived the Pulse Nightclub massacre in Orlando, Florida where 49 people died. He had been running from the Lord and lay there on the floor promising to live for the Lord the rest of his life. "Colon has kept his promise to God, traveling the world preaching about the freedom he has found in Jesus Christ. 'That promise was not easy at all, but look at today,' said Colon…Colon explained that the true meaning of deliverance and freedom is being able to look at temptation in the eye and say, 'I don't want you, I want Jesus'". [7]

The only way to look temptation in the eye and say, "I don't want you, I want Jesus" is to know Him as He is. When we begin to understand the grandeur, power, majesty and mercy of our great God, we will stand in awe of Him and desire to know Him and obey Him. If I have a caricature in my head of a God who moves on my behalf and ignores my sin, then I do not know the God of the Bible.

TIMELY TRUTH

The only way to change our actions is to change our thinking.

Samson is doing the same thing he has done before. He is falling for the same temptation and trap believing he will prevail. Only this time, his sin will lead to a much more devastating outcome.

Judges 16:20 records some of the saddest words in the Bible, "But he did not know that the Lord had departed from him." Samson has lost far more than his hair. He has lost the presence of God. The source of his strength was not his hair; the Source of his strength was God.

WEEK 9 » DAY FOUR » JUDGES 16:22-31

How the mighty Samson has fallen! His hair has been cut, his eyes have been gouged out, and he is shackled and grinding grain. All because of his unbridled passion. But, even still, God does not abandon him.

Read Judges 16:22-31.

1. What glimmer of hope for Samson is recorded in verse 22?

2. What god do the Philistines worship?

Dagon is the principle god of the Philistines. "Dagon was a West Semitic grain deity (cf. 1 Samuel 5:2-7; 1 Chronicles 10:10) adopted by the Philistines from the Amorites. Since they believed that their god had delivered Samson… into their hands…they called Samson out of the prison to entertain them (apparently expecting to see some acts of strength, or perhaps just to mock their now-powerless opponent)."[8]

3. Why do you think the Philistines bring Samson to Gaza?

4. Who are the Philistines really mocking as they mock Samson?

5. Why do you think God answers Samson's prayer in verse 28?

6. How many Philistines does Samson destroy in his death?

Samson's life is a sad commentary on the life of a chosen man of God. As we have seen, God's ways are not our ways (Isaiah 55:8-9). God chooses and uses people that we would not have chosen to accomplish His purposes. He is not limited by our disobedience, but oh how much we lose!

7. Fill in any remaining details about Samson on the chart on page 11.

As J.I. Packer writes,

> Consider the great price Samson paid to deliver his people temporarily from the oppression of the Philistines and how this points us forward to the one who delivered us not from the Philistines but from sin and death.[9]

8. Read 2 Corinthians 12:7-10. How can you apply this to your own life?

Early in our days of ministry, the Lord impressed upon me to memorize and apply in my life, Ephesians 3:20, "Now to Him who is able to do far more abundantly beyond all that we ask or think, according to the power that works within us."

9. What power works within us?

10. If the power of God's Spirit lives and works within us, is there anything that God has commanded that we are unable to accomplish?

I want to encourage you to begin praying Ephesians 3:20 and thanking God that your obedience is not dependent upon your own strength, but the strength of the Holy God who indwells you.

11. As you meditate upon this truth, how will it change your perspective of your current circumstances?

May we reflect on God's Word and apply it to our lives as we seek to live for Him until we see Him face to face.

WEEK 9 » DAY FIVE

1. What has happened to the culture of the Israelites as they have lived among idolatrous people?

2. Look back at the sin cycle that you began to fill out last week. Transfer your notes from last week on the sin cycle below and add the further details you have learned this week, noting the inevitable failure of the people to obey the Lord.

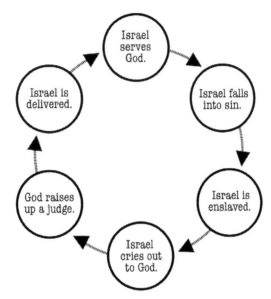

3. As you think about the post-Christian culture in which we live today, make a list of the idols that so often capture our hearts.

What is an idol? Tim Keller shares,

> It can be family and children, or career and making money, or achievement and critical acclaim, or saving 'face' and social standing. It can be a romantic relationship, peer approval, competence and skill, secure and comfortable circumstances, your beauty or your brains, a great political or social cause, your morality and virtue, or even success in the Christian ministry. When your meaning in life is to fix someone else's life we may call it 'co-dependency' but it is really idolatry. An idol is whatever you look at and say, in your heart of hearts, 'If I have that, then I'll feel my life has meaning, then I'll know I have value, then I'll feel significant and secure.' There are many ways to describe that kind of relationship to something, but perhaps the best one is worship. [10]

4. Can it be that when we live among idolatrous people that their values become our norm? How can we break free from an idolatrous mindset?

Our western secular culture has penetrated Christianity. Our desire for individual freedom often overrides what the Bible says about living in community and loving one another. We have a tendency to fall into the broken mindset that leads to rampant materialism, desire for power and success, an idolization of romantic love, and a focus on the external instead of the internal. This leads to a breakdown in the family and the church.

Tim Keller gives four ways we can assess our lives and thus our idols. Read through the following and honestly evaluate your own life.

1. Your imagination – "The true god of your heart is what your thoughts effortlessly go to when there is nothing else demanding our attention. What do you enjoy daydreaming about? What occupies your mind when you have nothing else to think about?"

2. Look at how you spend your money – "Jesus said, 'Where your treasure is, there is your heart also' (Matthew 6:21). Your money flows most effortlessly toward your heart's greatest love. In fact, the mark of an idol is that you spend too much money on it, and you must try to exercise self-control constantly."

3. Your faith in God – "What is your real, daily functional salvation? What are you really living for, what is your real – not your professed – god? A good way to discern this is how you respond to unanswered prayers and frustrated hopes."

4. Examine your most uncontrollable emotions – "Look for your idols at the bottom of your most painful emotions, especially those that never seem to lift and that drive you to do things you know are wrong. If you are angry, ask, 'Is there something here too important to me, something I must have at all costs?' Do the same thing with strong fear or despair and guilt."[11]

As we truthfully assess our own lives, we may have to draw some honest and sometimes painful conclusions. God allows pain for healing. Take what you have discovered to the Lord. Ask Him to help you root out anything that is competing for your heart's affections.

God's greatest command – "Love the Lord your God with all of your heart, and with all of your soul, and with all your mind, and with all your strength" (Mark 12:30) is for our greatest good! When my love for Christ surpasses my love for self, sin loses its hold. If I want to have victory over sin, I don't need to love myself less, but love Christ more.

TIMELY TRUTH

When my love for Christ surpasses my love for self, sin loses its hold.

When You Thought Things Couldn't Get Worse
Judges 17-21

*If only there were evil people somewhere insidiously committing evil deeds,
and it were necessary only to separate them from the rest of us and destroy them.
But the line dividing good and evil cuts through the heart of every human being.*[1]
~Aleksandr Solzhenitsyn

In 1919, at the conclusion of World War I, Irish poet William Butler Yeats penned a visionary poem on the future collapse of civilization, "The Second Coming". In the first stanza, Yeats writes,

> Things fall apart; the centre cannot hold;
> Mere anarchy is loosed upon the world,
> The ceremony of innocence is drowned;
> The best lack all conviction, while the worst
> Are full of passionate intensity.[2]

The first time I read this poem as a college student, it seemed prophetic. Decades later, it no longer seems like a prophecy, but a reality. A century after Yeats wrote his words, we are living in a time of pervasive moral decline, a time when mass killings and murders headline the news, a time when innocence has lost its value, and a time when those who should speak truth fail to do so for fear of being labeled intolerant. And all the while, the erosion of morality is reaching an advanced stage as things continue to "fall apart".

The last chapters of Judges give evidence to the fact that "the centre cannot hold" as the culture disintegrates. For the first sixteen chapters in Judges, we have watched the downward sin spiral of the Israelites on repeat. Beginning with Judges 17, the historical chronology of the book ends. The last five chapters are an appendix that record two case studies to illustrate the moral degeneracy of the period. Most Bible scholars believe that these two accounts actually occur earlier in the book, perhaps during the judgeship of Othniel, due to the mention of Jonathan, grandson of Moses in 18:30, the presence of Phinehas, son of Eleazar in 20:28, and the reference to the Ark of the Covenant being located at Bethel in 20:27-28. Together, the two stories we are going to study this week depict the religious apostasy, moral demise, and political anarchy that permeated the times.

WEEK 10 » DAY ONE » JUDGES 17

Read Judges 17:1-13.

The story of Micah, the lead character in this chapter, takes place during a time of moral relativism and widespread materialism.

1. What general statement is made regarding the times in which Micah lives in verse 6?

As we dig into the story of Micah, we are going to see that the moral decay of the times has invaded the foundations of the culture: the family, the church, and society. Dangerous times indeed. As the Psalmist writes, "If the foundations are destroyed, What can the righteous do?" (Psalm 11:3).

Decay in the Home

Micah's name means "Who is like Jehovah"[3], but as we will see, the correlation goes no deeper than his name.

2. What confession does Micah make to his mother? (v. 2)

When his mother finds out that it is her son who has stolen the money, she immediately tries to neutralize the curse she has pronounced, when the perpetrator was yet unknown, with a blessing.

3. What does Micah's mother do with the silver she dedicates to the Lord? (vv. 3-4)

We read in verse 5 that Micah already has a shrine where he keeps his household gods. Thanks to his mother's generosity, he now has another idol to add to his god collection.

4. Read Deuteronomy 12:1-8 and summarize God's laws about having a shrine (note the wording in verse 8).

5. And now to make familial matters even worse, who does Micah ordain to serve as the priest in his shrine? (Judges 17:5)

Remember, Micah and his mother are Israelites from the tribe of Ephraim, but they apparently know almost nothing about the Law God had given the Israelites to obey, an indicator of just how far Israel has strayed.

6. Read the Ten Commandments that God gave to Moses in Exodus 20:1-17 and make a list of the commandments that Micah and his mother (and presumably his son) have already broken by the time we get to verse 7.

TIMELY TRUTH

When people do what is right in their own eyes, they will end up doing what is wrong in God's eyes as they discard God's standard of truth and replace it with a norm of their own design.

Micah has now created his own unique homemade religion. He is aware that the Canaanites worshipped their gods with the aid of idols. In an act of religious syncretism, Micah has decided to mimic Canaanite worship practices, but not use them to worship Baal. He plans to worship Israel's God with the idols he has accumulated. Donald Campbell notes, "The tragedy of Micah's actions is intensified when we remember that Shiloh (the site of the tabernacle) was also in the hill country of Ephraim, probably only a short journey from the house of Micah." [4]

Decay in the Church

One day, a Levite from Bethlehem stops in to visit Micah's shrine. According to the Law, Levites are supposed to be supported by the offerings of the people (Numbers 18:8-32). The fact that this priest is having to wander through the area looking for a job points to the apostasy that has crept into the Israelites' religious practices. When Micah meets the wandering priest, he immediately sees a way to take his shrine to the next level—a real Levite priest.

7. What compensation package does Micah offer the Levite? (v. 10)

The young Levite readily takes Micah up on his offer and becomes a private priest, a hireling, a Levite concierge. Together, he and Micah make up their own rules for worship instead of following those that had been laid out in detail in the Law. By creating their own standard of religious conduct, they take it upon themselves to determine their own standard of right and wrong, subjectivity that characterizes spiritual relativism during the dark times of Judges. When people do what is right in their own eyes, they will end up doing what is wrong in God's eyes as they discard God's standard of truth and replace it with a norm of their own design.

8. In verse 13, we see the motivation behind Micah's house church. What are his expectations of God?

Warren Wiersbe observes,

> The sad part of the story is that Micah now thought he had the favor of God because a genuine Levitical priest was serving as his private chaplain. Micah practiced a false religion and worshipped false gods (with Jehovah thrown in for good measure), and all the while he rested on the false confidence that God was blessing him![5]

9. Read John 4:23-24. Contrast Micah's religious activity with that of true worshipers.

Spend a few minutes with the Lord thinking about how He wants us to worship Him. Do you worship according to the truth of Scripture? Is your worship centered in God? Is there any place where false worship has seeped in?

> *Worship is a meeting at the center so that our lives are centered in God and not lived eccentrically.*
> *We worship so that we live in response to and from this center, the living God.*
> *Failure to worship consigns us to a life of spasms and jerks,*
> *at the mercy of every advertisement, every seduction, every siren.*
> *Without worship we live manipulated and manipulating lives.*
> *We move in either frightened panic or deluded lethargy as we are,*
> *in turn, alarmed by specters and soothed by placebos.*
> *If there is no center, there is no circumference.*[6]
> ~Eugene Peterson

Without true worship, the center cannot hold.

WEEK 10 » DAY TWO » JUDGES 18

A pilgrim of the mid-twentieth century, C. S. Lewis witnessed the mounting moral decay and intellectual deterioration of Western civilization. In his book, *The Abolition of Man*, Lewis points out that the products of relativism–the belief that there are no absolute truths–are waning morality and an absence of virtue. He explains that when a society fails to believe in and teach universal moral laws, we ignore the education of the heart and are left with intelligent men and women who act like animals or in his words, "men without chests," those who without a moral compass are controlled by their appetites. When the heart is ignored, Lewis explains, "In a sort of ghastly simplicity we remove the organ and demand the function. We make men without chests and expect of them virtue and enterprise. We laugh at honour and are shocked to find traitors in our midst."[7]

Micah's story in Judges 18-19 illustrates the powerful inclination within the human heart to spiral downward into sinful behavior and do whatever is "right in his own eyes" (Judges 17:6). Micah has accumulated idols, built a shrine, and employed a Levite priest, but he has failed to conform to God's truth. By ignoring his heart, Micah has become a man "without a chest," someone with an outward religion who is empty inside. Micah is assured that his outward performance is going to win him the favor of God. He can sense change in the air. And things are about to change, but not in the way Micah is expecting.

Decay in Society

Read Judges 18:1-31.

1. What is the setting for the rest of Micah's story? (v. 1)

Never has a statement been more true than the beginning of verse 1, "Israel had no king" (NIV). That sad condition was one of their own making. They should have been worshiping God as their Faithful King. His Word should have been their law. But they were determined to do their own thing their own way.

The tribe of Dan gives us a glimpse into the rebellion against God, which prevailed during the time of the Judges.

2. Read the following verses and make notes on what you learn about the tribe of Dan, descendants from Jacob's fifth son (Genesis 30:5-6).

   Numbers 1:39

   Joshua 19:40-48

   Judges 1:34

3. Why is the tribe of Dan looking for a place to live?

Donald Campbell notes,

> Even though they had a military potential of 64,400 men (Numbers 26:43), they were unable to occupy the territory allocated to them (Joshua 19:41-46; Judges 1:34). Their failure to drive out the Ammonites was due not to a lack of power but to a lack of faith. The tribe therefore had two choices: to repent of their unbelief and claim the promise of God as they battled their enemies, or to look for a new territory where the occupants would be unprepared and vulnerable to attack. The tribe of Dan chose the easy way, but it was not the way of faith.[8]

Mimicking the conquering of Canaan when Joshua sent out 12 spies, the Danites send out spies to look for a home for their tribe.

4. Summarize the conversation that takes place between Micah's priest and the spies from Dan. (vv. 3-6)

5. Is there any godly significance in the blessing the priest gives in verse 6?

6. Find Laish in the area north of the Sea of Galilee on the map on page 7. Why do the spies choose Laish? (v. 7)

7. As the 600 Danites begin their quest to conquer Laish, what happens when they come to Micah's house? (vv. 14-20)

Micah, the man who stole from his mother, is in despair when he realizes that his idols and his priest have been taken from him. He has placed his trust in his idol collection, but they can do nothing to help him as he stands by and watches the Danites haul them away.

8. Compare Micah's words in verse 24 with the Psalmist's words in Psalm 73:25-26.

After an unsuccessful attempt to recapture his idols, Micah returns back home empty handed. Loaded up with idols and a corrupt priest, the Danites proceed with their takeover plan of Laish. Greed is the underlying motivation for every character in this story. Micah built his shrine and filled it with idols because he wanted more. The Levite priest once again says yes to the highest bidder because he wants more. The Danites are about to go to war against a peaceable people because they want more.

9. What happens when the Danites reach Laish?

Greed gives way to violence and murder revealing the wickedness of the human heart. So it should be no surprise to us that the Danites create a culture devoid of God and set up an idolatrous system of religion using Micah's idols and Micah's priest. The writer of Judges has saved an interesting detail about the Levite priest until verse 30.

10. Read Exodus 2:21-22 to help fill in some additional information about Jonathan, the young Levite who becomes a priest for hire.

One sad subplot to Micah's story is the young Levite priest. He is a man who has God's calling on His life, but is more concerned about self-promotion than seeking God. And in the end, he has become the apostate priest of an entire tribe and bears the responsibility for leading them into idolatry. When the writer reveals the priest's identity, the depth of spiritual anarchy that has taken place becomes evident. Jonathan is the son of Gershom and a descendent of Moses. In Judges 18:30, some translations indicate that Gershom is the son of Manasseh; others say he is the son of Moses. Gary Inrig explains:

> …Manasseh is a scribal attempt to avoid the embarrassment of what the Hebrew text really says. The text reveals that Jonathan was a descendant of the great Moses. To cover the fact that such a godly man could have so worthless a descendant, the scribes altered his name. But it is a stark reminder that it does not do any good to have a godly ancestor if you do not know God yourself. Godliness is not genetic.[9]

This young priest is an example of what happens when our service becomes more about ourselves than it does God. As John Piper admonishes, "We may think we are centering our lives on God when we are really making Him a means to self-esteem." [10] It is fitting for us to regularly evaluate our motivation for service by asking, "am I serving God or am I serving self?"

A second subplot that serves as a perpetual warning against idolatry is the rest of the story for the tribe of Dan. The tribe is not mentioned in the genealogies of 1 Chronicles, nor are they mentioned in Revelation 7 among the 144,000 Hebrew believers who will carry out a special ministry for God during the Tribulation. The tribe of Dan left God out of their lives and became a sorrowful illustration of Proverbs 14:12, "There is a way which seems right to a man, But its end is the way of death."

In losing, spend a few minutes reflecting on what we have studied today. More than seventy years have passed since Lewis wrote *The Abolition of Man* and things have gotten undeniably worse. Western civilization is experiencing moral collapse, societal chaos, and cultural decay in epidemic proportions. Are there any places where the culture has crept in to your heart? Has any form of idolatry taken root?

David Powlison writes about the danger of encroaching idolatry,

> ...[the] most basic question which God continually poses to each human heart: Has something or someone besides Jesus the Christ taken title to your heart's trust, preoccupation, loyalty, service, fear, and delight? It is a question bearing on the immediate motivation of one's behavior, thoughts, and feelings. In the Bible's conceptualization, the motivation question is the lordship question: who or what "rules" my behavior, the Lord or an idol? [11]

Our focused determination to live as people with chests—strong hearts filled with God's truth and ruled solely by Him—sets us apart from our society. As our lives become the "fragrance of Christ" (2 Corinthians 2:15), the world will take notice and be pointed to "the hope" that is within us (1 Peter 3:15).

WEEK 10 » DAY THREE » JUDGES 19

If you have ever made the trip from Chattanooga to Knoxville via I-75, you know it is absolutely breathtaking. Flanked by beautiful mountain panoramas and winding rivers, it is one of the most picturesque drives in the eastern United States. But on the morning of December 11, 1990, this scenic area became the location of the worst traffic accident in Tennessee history. The area is prone to dense fog, especially during the early morning hours near the Hiawassee River. Just after 9 a.m. on that brisk December morning, visibility near the Calhoun, Tennessee exit dropped to less than ten feet.

When the driver of a tractor-trailer truck slowed down in the southbound lane of I-75, a second truck crashed into it. While the two drivers were inspecting their trucks, an automobile crashed into the rear truck, and in turn was hit by another big rig causing a fire that quickly began to spread. Meanwhile, other collisions began occurring in the northbound lanes. By the time it was over, ninety-nine cars were involved in disastrous chain reaction collisions. Twelve people died and forty-two were injured. The National Transportation Safety Board concluded that the cause of the collisions was varying driver response to the reduced visibility caused by fog.[12]

We are living in a time when a dense moral fog has settled upon society. Ethical and moral boundaries that were once the standard have not just been blurred; they have been completely obliterated. Everywhere we look, this moral fog is the basis for people doing what is right in their own eyes. The last story in Judges is an example of what happens when we live that way. Be warned though, what we are about to study is the most horrific instance of moral degradation in Scripture:

> In many ways the last section of Judges is the sewer of Scripture. It holds the dubious distinction of being the most disgusting and degraded story in the Bible, unredeemed by an admirable character or moral act. To read these chapters is to be repelled by them, and you cannot help feeling rather dirty. It is almost as bad as reading a newspaper today. That is not an exaggeration, but a reminder that the awful degradation that blotched Israel's history is an everyday occurrence in our society. Perhaps that is why God allowed this story to be recorded. After all, the Spirit who inspired Scripture is the Holy Spirit. He did not give us this story to shock our sensibilities, but to teach us truth.[13]

Judges 19:1 once again begins with the ominous refrain, "Now it came about in those days, when there was no king in Israel…" Because the Israelites were viewing their situation through their own eyes, they believed that they had no king. But they did have a King. He was simply ignored and forgotten. They had forgotten that God had established Israel as a theocracy with Him as King. He wanted them to obey His rules and submit to His reign. The declaration that there is no king in Israel is evidence that they are not submitting to Him and the catastrophic result is spiritual and moral mayhem. As he frames the setting for this era, the writer is foreshadowing the dark events that are to follow.

However, no amount of foreshadowing can really prepare us for the sordid tale we are about to read.

Read Judges 19:1-30.

Again, a Levite plays a lead role in the story.

1. Read Numbers 3:6-9 and summarize the responsibilities of a Levite.

Levites were set apart by God to do His work and uphold God's standard of holiness. However, this Levite has been influenced by culture and has taken a concubine. In ancient Israel, a concubine was considered to be a second-class wife. She had most of the duties of a wife, but few of the privileges. The Life Application Bible notes, "Although she was legally attached to one man, she and her children usually did not have the inheritance rights of the legal wife and legitimate children. Her primary purpose was giving the man sexual pleasure, bearing additional children, and contributing more help to the household or estate."[14] The practice of having a concubine, while common, was not intended by God (Genesis 2:24) and was not divinely sanctioned.

2. Where is the Levite from? (v. 1)

3. Where is his concubine's hometown? (vv. 1-2)

4. Describe the hospitality the girl's father offers to the Levite. (vv. 3-9)

One commentary explains,

> The father's generosity may appear exaggerated or overbearing to a western audience, but his actions are perfectly consistent with the experience of people from most of the two-thirds world, especially Middle Eastern countries. Hospitality was and still is a most important cultural value, and any deficiency in fulfilling one's obligations was/is looked upon as grossly shameful, even sinful. [15]

In verses 11-12, the Levite refuses to stop for the night in Jebus because the city belongs to foreigners, another group of pagans that the Israelites have failed to drive out of the land. So the group travels on to Gibeah, an Israelite town a few miles north of Bethlehem. The extravagant hospitality of the girl's father is strikingly different from the welcome they receive in Gibeah.

5. What tribe lives in Gibeah? (v. 14)

6. Recount the details of what happens in Gibeah. (vv 15-26)

As you read this account, no doubt, bells went off as your mind made the connection between the account in Judges 19 and the story of Sodom and Gomorrah in Genesis 19.

7. Read Genesis 19. What parallels do you see between the two stories?

Israel has now become so Canaanized that their behavior mirrors that of the inhabitants of Sodom.

As I read the abhorrent incident in Judges 19, several questions come to mind:

- Why does the old man protect the Levite at the expense of the woman who is a guest in his home? (Not to mention his willingness to include his daughter in the sickening negotiation.)

- What depth of cowardice and sin would cause the Levite to be willing to sacrifice the woman he professes to love to save his own self?

- Since when is the gang rape of a woman preferable to homosexual assault? (Both are horrible.)

And the apparent answer is that Israel has drifted so far away from God's Law that the total moral structure within the nation has crumbled leaving them with nothing but the ruins of utter depravity. The progressive Canaanization of Israel has taken hold. Until this point, something this vile would have only taken place in Sodom among the Canaanites—now this barbaric atrocity is being committed by the people of God. No longer is there a line of demarcation between God's people and the Canaanites. Or the Sodomites. No. Difference. At. All.

8. Read Judges 19:26-29 and think about the actions of the Levite as you do. How do his actions reveal the depth to which immorality has penetrated Israel?

Note that the concubine is never called by her name. She has no rights. She is chattel, not a cherished bride. Katie McCoy recently posted this observation on Twitter:

> Beginning of Judges: A woman has a name, a voice, is heard and honored. [Think Deborah and Jael]
>
> End of Judges: A woman is nameless, voiceless, is silenced, and dehumanized.
>
> The greater a culture's moral decline, the less it values the voice, personhood, and humanity of women. [16]

The account recorded in Judges 19 is what happens when a nation loses its conscience. Do you see any similarities between America in 2019 and Israel during the days of the Judges?

Israel was in a moral fog; it had lost its moral bearings. What about America?

Israel was a nation where everyone did what was right in his or her own eyes. What about America?

In Israel, there had been too little personal encounter with the living God. Too much darkness. Not enough light. Due to compromise and carnality, God's people blended in with their pagan neighbors. What about America?

Israel's departure from God's standard had occurred slowly, so most people were not even aware of how far they had drifted. What about America?

Is there hope?

In his book, *The Signature of Jesus*, Brennan Manning pointedly states that the hope for the world lies in believers having a fresh encounter with Jesus:

> If indeed we lived a life in imitation of His, our witness would be irresistible. If we dared to live beyond our self-concern, if we refused to shrink from being vulnerable, if we took nothing but a compassionate attitude toward the world, if we were a counterculture to our nation's lunatic lust for pride of place, power, and possessions, if we preferred to be faithful rather than successful, the walls of indifference to Jesus Christ would crumble. A handful of us could be ignored by society, but hundreds, thousands, millions of such servants would overwhelm the world. Christians filled with the authenticity, commitment, and generosity of Jesus would be the most spectacular sign in the history of the human race. The call of Jesus is revolutionary. If we implemented it, we would change the world in a few months.[17]

It is past time for believers to live beyond ourselves–to stand up, speak out, and overwhelm the world with the revolutionary, life-changing nature of the gospel. And when we do, the fog will begin to lift.

Virtue–even attempted virtue–brings light; indulgence brings fog.[18]
~C. S. Lewis

WEEK 10 » DAY FOUR » JUDGES 20

At the end of yesterday's study, did you find yourself wondering why the Levite sends his concubine's body parts throughout Israel? It certainly couldn't be because he is mourning her death. After all, he was the one who sent her out to the men. In fact, his complicit actions make him an accomplice. What is his motivation? Revenge. He has lost a piece of property and he wants the men from Gibeah to pay. The Levite hopes that the tribes of Israel will be shocked into action when they receive evidence of the horrific crime. And his plan has just the effect he wanted. Eleven tribes unite and meet at Mizpah, just a few miles north of Gibeah. (Judges 20:3 indicates that the tribe of Benjamin did not attend.)

Read Judges 20:1-11.

1. Briefly summarize what took place during the convocation at Mizpah.

2. What details does the murdered concubine's husband edit out of his self-serving testimony? (vv. 4-7)

After hearing the Levite's statement, the people of Israel deliver a unanimous verdict. The men from Gibeah are guilty. Since Gibeah is a city of Benjamin, the Israelites send representatives to the Benjamites and demand that the criminals be delivered for judgment.

Read Judges 20:12-17.

3. How does the tribe of Benjamin respond to the ultimatum to turn over the guilty men? (vv. 13-14)

When sin isn't exposed, confessed, and punished, it pollutes society and defiles the land.[19]
~Warren Wiersbe

Benjamin is so committed to protecting the criminals in their midst that they meet at Gibeah and declare civil war against the rest of the tribes of Israel. Why do the Benjamites not just turn the guilty men over to be punished? Tim Keller explains,

> One idol that is most destructive to human unity is the idol of our blood or kindred; the attitude of my family/country, right or wrong. Though common decency tells us that the men of Gibeah had violated all moral standards, the Benjamites close ranks and refuse to allow any outsiders to find fault with any insiders. When we put our blood or racial ties or community above the common good and the transcendent moral order, we make a god of "our own" people.[20]

The Israelites decide that their 400,000 soldiers are more than what is needed to defeat the 26,700 Benjamite troops and decide to send one out of every ten (chosen by lot) into battle.

Read Judges 20:18-28.

Similar to Judges 1:1-2, the Israelites go to Bethel to inquire of God which tribe should lead the attack (v. 18). Both times, God responds that Judah should be the tribe to lead into battle. However, there are two differences between the accounts in Judges 1 and Judges 20. One is that in Judges 1:1-2, they are fighting the Canaanites; in Judges 20, they are going up against God's people. The same Israel that would not unite in battle against the Canaanites, the Midianites, or the Ammonites finally unites, but tragically, it is to fight against itself. The second difference is that when they are going to fight the Canaanites, God guarantees success (Judges 1:2); when they are fighting brother against brother, God does not promise victory (Judges 20:18).

4. Who wins the first two battles? (vv. 21, 25)

After both defeats, Israel goes to Bethel to seek God. Although the tabernacle is still at Shiloh, the Ark has been brought down to Bethel, just five miles from Mizpah. After their second defeat, they spend an entire day weeping, fasting, and sacrificing burnt offerings and peace offerings. Donald Campbell notes, "While Israel's two defeats are not explicitly explained, the defeats indicate that though Benjamin had sinned greatly, the other tribes were not without sin, and God's judgment had fallen on them." [21] The sacrifices do not make the Israelites better fighters; they make them right with the God who will now fight for them (Exodus 14:14; Deuteronomy 1:30). Note: This is the only time the Ark of the Covenant is mentioned in Judges, demonstrating how seldom the Israelites consulted God.

5. In response to their true repentance, what does the Lord promise the Israelites will happen the next day? (v. 28)

Read Judges 20:29-48.

The third battle is described twice in these verses. A general account is given in verses 29-36a, followed by a more detailed account in verses 36b-46.

6. What happens during the third day of battle? (vv. 29-48)

The judgment on the tribe of Benjamin is a commentary on the wages of sin. By the end of the battle, 25,100 from the tribe of Benjamin were killed; only 600 remained. But the Benjamites were not the only ones who suffered consequences. Israel lost 40,000 men (ten percent of their army). (If you are doing the math here, you may question an unaccounted for loss of 1000 Benjamites. Commentators believe these men died in earlier battles.)

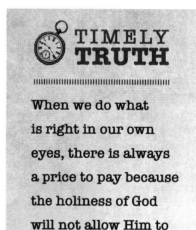

TIMELY TRUTH

When we do what is right in our own eyes, there is always a price to pay because the holiness of God will not allow Him to accommodate sin.

Pause for a moment and think about the standard practice of doing "what was right in their own eyes" during the period of the Judges. The account in Judges 19-20 is the most appalling example of this form of arrogance:

- The men of Gibeah decided that rape was acceptable.

- The farmer and the Levite believed that homosexual rape was wrong, but condoned the rape of a woman.

- The tribe of Benjamin overlooked sin and defended perverse men.

- Israel determined that retaliation and revenge was justifiable.

When we do what is right in our own eyes, there is always a price to pay because the holiness of God will not allow Him to accommodate sin. A. W. Tozer writes,

> Holy is the way God is. To be holy He does not conform to a standard. He is that standard. He is absolutely holy with an infinite, incomprehensible fullness of purity that is incapable of being other than it is. Because He is holy, all His attributes are holy; that is, whatever we think of as belonging to God must be thought of as holy.
>
> God is holy and He has made holiness the moral condition necessary to the health of His universe. Sin's temporary presence in the world only accents this. Whatever is holy is healthy; evil is a moral sickness that must end ultimately in death. [22]

When we live according to what is right in our own eyes, we lose our awareness of the holiness of God. Soon, we find that sin ravages our spirit, twists our soul, and "reduces us to little more than animals, living as mere bodies, with our humanity almost erased."[23] This is exactly what happened in Judges 19-20. And it is what is happening in the twenty-first century.

Has the "do what is right in your own eyes" mindset crept into your life? Do you find yourself excusing certain sins in your life?

7. Close out your time in God's Word today by reflecting upon Isaiah's response to his sin when he encounters the holiness of God in Isaiah 6:1-7. Note how Isaiah's response is different from the Israelites during the time of the Judges. Does your personal response to sin mirror the prophet's acknowledgment of sin or the Israelites?

WEEK 10 » DAY FIVE » JUDGES 21

Just when you thought things couldn't get worse in this awful episode, they do. Like a single spark can trigger a raging forest fire that consumes thousands of acres, the initial inhospitality in the Gibeah town square launches a series of events that deteriorates rapidly. Rape, murder, dismemberment, and civil war result, and now the eleven tribes of Israel are faced with a dreadful dilemma as the twelfth tribe faces near extinction.

Read Judges 21:1-14.

1. What vow did the other tribes of Israel make at Mizpah regarding the tribe of Benjamin? (v. 1)

After the civil war, only 600 Benjamite men remain. Their wives and families have all been killed. Even though this predicament is of their own making, the Israelites are grieved that one of their tribes is in danger of eradication. Because of the vow they have taken, they cannot offer any of their daughters in marriage to the Benjamites and marrying Gentile women is not an option. But then, they recall the second vow they took at Mizpah.

2. What is the second vow that the Israelites made at Mizpah? (v. 5)

3. What people do the Israelites discover had not attended the assembly at Mizpah? (vv. 8-9)

The Israelites devise a plan that will allow them to keep their first vow without the tribe of Benjamin being exterminated. They will keep their second vow! So they send a regiment of 12,000 to Jabesh-Gilead to kill every man, woman, and child. (Note that once again, the Israelites are waging war against themselves rather than fighting the wicked Canaanites.) The only exception is that young women who are virgins will be spared. When the Israelites return to

Shiloh, they bring 400 virgins to be given to the surviving men of Benjamin. Now, where will they find wives for the other 200 men?

Read Judges 21:15-25.

4. What is the next plot the Israel elders concoct to solve the problem without violating the oath they have made regarding their daughters? (vv. 15-22)

5. How do the elders instruct the Benjamites to acquire their wives? (vv. 20-21)

6. What do the men from the tribe of Benjamin do? (vv 22-24)

Wait just a minute. Aren't these women daughters of Israelites? What about the vow? Although the men from the other eleven tribes have taken an oath that none of their daughters could be "given" in marriage to a man from the tribe of Benjamin, the elders decide that nothing had been said in the vow about a daughter being "taken" by a Benjamite. The conclusion is that it will be acceptable for a man from the tribe of Benjamin to kidnap an Israelite daughter during the festival. Acceptable, that is, by the standards of the day. And not only are these 200 virgin daughters kidnapped, the Israelites then twist the law so that the women are kept as a wives:

> If a man finds a girl who is a virgin, who is not engaged, and seizes her and lies with her and they are discovered, then the man who lay with her shall give to the girl's father fifty shekels of silver, and she shall become his wife because he has violated her; he cannot divorce her all his days. ~Deuteronomy 22:28-29

The same men who went to war with the tribe of Benjamin over the rape of the concubine in Judges 19-20 have actually devised a plan that includes the authorized rape of 200 Israelite virgins by the remnant of Benjamin. Are you shaking your head at the depth of perversion this saga has reached?

When the compound effect of sin infiltrates a nation, the result is moral rot.

How is it that God's people find themselves at this point?

7. Turn back and look at Judges 20:27-28 to gain some insight. Where is the Ark of the Covenant located at this time?

Gary Inrig explains the significance of the Ark being at Bethel instead of being housed in the tabernacle in Shiloh:

> From Joshua, Judges, and 1 Samuel, we know that the tabernacle was in Shiloh, and the Ark of the Covenant belonged in the Holy of Holies of the tabernacle in Shiloh. The ark was intensely holy, and no one was to view it, except the high priest once a year. But the holiness of God had been so cheapened that the high priest had allowed it to be taken out of the tabernacle and transported to Bethel, in direct disobedience to God. What makes this doubly sad is that the priest was Phineas, a man who once stood powerfully for God (see Numbers 25). That is the root of all sin–a weak conception of the holiness of God.[24]

The Israelites have been so concerned about following the letter of their man-made vow that they have failed to keep the spirit of God's holy law. Consequently, the moral fiber of Israel has been utterly lost.

8. What editorial comment does the writer make in verse 25?

Israel has no earthly king, but not once do they go before God, their Faithful King, about their plan to repopulate the tribe of Benjamin.

9. In what ways are we just like Israel, prone to lean into our own understanding, to follow our own plans, without acknowledging Him or seeking Him?

As the hymn writer says, we are "prone to wander" and "prone to leave the God [we] love." [25]

Here is the overarching message of Judges. Mankind is unfaithful. But. God is faithful.

The unfaithfulness of man. Judges illustrates that mankind, even at its "best", is unfaithful. What we think is often wrong. What we do is often evil. What we worship is often idolatrous. Unfaithfulness is at the core of our sinful DNA. We cannot save ourselves. We cannot rule ourselves.

We need a King to save us. A heavenly King.

The faithfulness of God. Throughout Judges, we repeatedly see the depth of God's faithfulness to save His children. Through His redemptive plan, God's faithfulness swallows up our unfaithfulness.

> Jesus sought me when a stranger
> Wandering from the fold of God
> He, to rescue me from danger
> Interposed His precious blood.[26]

Jesus, the Better Judge, (Hebrews 12:24) has provided a way for us, messed up people with messed up lives, to be restored. All who come to Him in repentance receive a new heart. By His grace, He reverses the penalty of our sin and we are "born again to a living hope" (1 Peter 1:3). If you have never surrendered your heart and life to Christ, please do not read any further without doing so. In the appendix of this study you will find a guide that will walk you through the steps to invite Christ into your life.

As we have come to the end of this study, please turn the page in your Bible. You will find that the next book is Ruth and it begins with these words, "Now it came about in the days when the judges governed…" The story of Ruth is a breath of fresh air, a respite from the epilogue we have just finished. In fact, it is really difficult to believe that this magnificent story of redemption occurs during the time of the judges. But it does! "It was the best of times, it was the worst of times…" is not merely a line from a Dickens' classic; these words capture Ruth's story of redemption in the midst of ruin.

Ruth doesn't hold a prestigious position nor does she come from a well-known, godly family. She is a widow from an enemy nation (Moab) with no prospects for marriage. Her story of redemption continues the theme of God's faithfulness in dark times. It demonstrates God's steadfast love and undeserved kindness to His people. Ruth's story is a reminder of what can happen when one woman yields her life to God, even when times are dark.

How has God spoken to you through this study? What have you learned about Him? What have you discovered about yourself? God wants to use your story of redemption to be a light in these dark times. Just as in the time of the judges, the problem today is not the presence of darkness. It's the absence of light. Will you be light?

You're here to be light, bringing out the God-colors in the world. God is not a secret to be kept.
We're going public with this, as public as a city on a hill. If I make you light-bearers,
you don't think I'm going to hide you under a bucket, do you? I'm putting you on a light stand.
Now that I've put you there on a hilltop, on a light stand—shine!
Matthew 5:14-15, MSG

How to Become a Christian

Dear one, has there ever been a time that you have given your heart to the Lord? Do you have the assurance that if you were to die right now, you would go straight to heaven to spend all eternity in the presence of the Lord Jesus Christ and all His followers? If not, please let me share with you how you can be saved.

Admit Your Sin

First, you must understand that you are a sinner. The Bible says, *All have sinned and fall short of the glory of God* (Rom. 3:23). In Romans 6:23 the Bible says, *For the wages of sin is death.* That means that sin has separated us from a Holy God and we are under the sentence of eternal death and separation from God.

Abandon Self-Effort

Secondly, you must understand that you cannot save yourself by your own efforts. The Bible is very clear that it is *not by works of righteousness which we have done, but according to His mercy He saved us* (Titus 3:5). Again, in Ephesians 2:8-9 the Bible says, *For by grace you have been saved through faith; and that not of yourselves, it is the gift of God; not as a result of works, that no one should boast.*

Acknowledge Christ's Payment

Thirdly, you must believe that Jesus Christ, the Son of God, died for your sins. The Bible says, *God demonstrates His own love toward us, in that while we were yet sinners, Christ died for us* (Rom. 5:8). That means He died a sacrificial death in your place. Your sin debt has been paid by the blood of Jesus Christ, which *cleanses us from all sin* (I John 1:7).

Accept Him as Savior

Fourthly, you must put your faith in Jesus Christ and Him alone for your salvation. The blood of Christ does you no good until you receive Him by faith. The Bible says, *Believe on the Lord Jesus Christ, and you shall be saved* (Acts 16:31).

Has there been a time in your life that you have taken this all-important step of faith? If not, I urge you to do it right now. Jesus Christ is the only way to heaven. He said, *"I am the way, the truth, and the life; no man comes unto the Father, but by Me"* (John 14:16).

Would you like to become a Christian? Would you like to invite Jesus Christ to come into your heart today? Read over this prayer and if it expresses the desire of your heart, you may ask Him into your heart to take away your sin, fill you with His Spirit, and take you to home to heaven when you die. If this is your intention, pray this prayer.

"Oh God, I'm a sinner. I am lost and I need to be saved. I know I cannot save myself, so right now, once and for all, I trust You to save me. Come into my heart, forgive my sin, and make me Your child. I give you my life. I will live for You as You give me Your strength. Amen"

If you will make this your heartfelt prayer, God will hear and save you! Jesus has promised that He will never leave nor forsake anyone who comes to Him in faith. In John 6:37 He said, *"The One who comes to Me I will certainly not cast out."*

Welcome to the family!

End Notes

Introduction

1. Sorokowski, A. (1988). *Christian History Institute.* Retrieved from https://christianhistoryinstitute.org/magazine/article/russian-christianity-and-the-revolution-what-happened

2. Sorokowski, A. (1988). *Christian History Institute.* Retrieved from https://christianhistoryinstitute.org/magazine/article/russian-christianity-and-the-revolution-what-happened

3. Sorokowski, A. (1988). *Christian History Institute.* Retrieved from https://christianhistoryinstitute.org/magazine/article/russian-christianity-and-the-revolution-what-happened

4. Solzhenitsyn, A. (2018). *The National Review.* Retrieved from https://www.nationalreview.com/2018/12/aleksandr-solzhenitsyn-men-have-forgotten-god-speech/

5. Solzhenitsyn, A. (2018). *The National Review.* Retrieved from https://www.nationalreview.com/2018/12/aleksandr-solzhenitsyn-men-have-forgotten-god-speech/

6. MacArthur, J. (2016). *Joshua, Judges & Ruth: Finally in the Land,* p. vii. Nashville, TN: Nelson Books.

7. MacArthur, J. (2016). *Joshua, Judges & Ruth: Finally in the Land,* p. vii. Nashville, TN: Nelson Books.

8. Campbell, D.K. (1989). *Judges: Leaders in Christ Times,* p. 11. Wheaton, IL: Victor Books.

9. Arnold, B.T. & Beyer, B.E. (1998). *Encountering The Old Testament,* p. 186. Grand Rapids, MI: Baker Books.

10. Wood, L. (1975). *Distressing Days of the Judges,* p. 2 Grand Rapids, MI: Zondervan Publishing.

Week 1

1. Packer, J. I. (2018). *Judges: A 12-Week Study,* p. 7. Wheaton, IL: Crossway.

2. Slattery, Julie. (2018). *Rethinking Sexuality,* p. 37. New York, NY: Multnomah.

3. Keller, T. (2013). *Judges For You,* p. 9. UK: The Good Book Company.

4. Bonhoeffer, Dietrich. (1953). *Temptation,* p. 33. New York, NY: SCM Press.

5. Keller, T. (2013). *Judges for You,* p. 167. UK: The Good Book Company.

6. Keller, T. (2013). *Judges For You,* p. 19. UK: The Good Book Company.

7. Keller, T. (2013). *Judges For You,* p. 23. UK: The Good Book Company.

8. Keller, T. (2013). *Judges For You,* p. 31. UK: The Good Book Company.

9. Willard, D. (2014). *Living in Christ's Presence*, p. 16. Downers Grove, IL: Intervarsity Press.

Week 2

1. Guinness, O. (1992). *No God but God*, p. 32-33. Moody Press.

2. Campbell, D. (1989). *Judges: Leaders in Crisis Times*, p.11. Wheaton, IL: SP Publications, Inc.

3. Beldman, D. (2017). *Deserting the King: The Book of Judges*, p. 23. Bellingham, WA: Lexham Press.

4. Keller, T. (2013). *Judges for You*, p. 38. UK: The Good Book Company.

5. Wiersbe, W. (1994). *Be Available*, p. 23. Wheaton, Illinois: Victor Books.

6. Brensinger, T.L. (1999). *Judges*, p.43-44. Scottdale, PA: Herald Press.

7. Ridout, S. (2015 Kindle Edition). *Judges and Ruth*. Ontario, Canada: Believer's Bookshelf.

8. Keller, T. (2013). *Judges for You*, p.10. UK: The Good Book Company.

9. Wiersbe, W. (1994). *Be Available*, p. 25. Wheaton, Illinois: Victor Books.

10. Chambers, O. (1935). *My Utmost For His Highest*, p. 79. Grand Rapids, MI: Dodd, Mead & Company, Inc.

11. Ingrid, G. (1979). *Hearts of Iron, Feet of Clay*, p. 52. Chicago, IL: Moody Press.

12. Wiersbe, W. (1994). *Be Available*, p. 21. Wheaton, IL: Victor Books.

13. Keller, T. (2009). *Counterfeit Gods: The Empty Promises of Money, Sex, and Power, and the Only Hope that Matters*, p. 171. New York, New York: Penguin Books.

14. MacArthur, J. (2016). *Joshua, Judges, and Ruth: Finally, in the Land*, p. 68. Nashville, TN: Nelson Books.

Week 3

1. Emerson, R. W. (n.d.). Ralph Waldo Emerson Quotes. *Goodreads*, Retrieved from https://www.goodreads.com/quotes/64541-the-purpose-of-life-is-not-to-be-happy-it

2. James, C. C. (2005). *Lost Women of the Bible*, p. 43. Grand Rapids, MI: Zondervan

3. James, C. C. (2005). *Lost Women of the Bible*, p. 30. Grand Rapids, MI: Zondervan.

4. James, C. C. (2005). *Lost Women of the Bible*, p. 37-38. Grand Rapids, MI: Zondervan.

5. James, C. C. (2005). *Lost Women of the Bible*, p. 43. Grand Rapids, MI: Zondervan.

6. Inrig, G. (1979). *Hearts of Iron, Feet of Clay*, p. 58. Chicago, IL: Moody Press.

7. Keller, T. (2013). *Judges for You*, p. 54. UK: The Good Book Company.

8. Keller, T. (2013). *Judges for You*, p. 58. UK: The Good Book Company.

9. Keller, T. (2013). *Judges for You*, p. 55. UK: The Good Book Company.

10. Keller, T. (2013). *Judges for You*, p. 55-56. UK: The Good Book Company.

11. Keller, T. (2013). *Judges for You*, p. 56. UK: The Good Book Company.

12. Zodhiates, S., ed. (1996). *The Hebrew-Greek Key Word Study Bible*, p. 1512. Chattanooga, TN: AMG Publishers.

13. Lancaster, D. T. *Miracles of the Six-Day War*. Retrieved from https://ffoz.org/discover/messiah-magazine/miracles-of-the-six-day-war.html

14. Davis, D. R. (1990). *Such a Great Salvation*, p. 79. Grand Rapids, MI: Baker Book House Company.

15. Keller, Timothy. (2013). *Judges for You*, p. 61-62. UK: The Good Book Company.

16. Martin, J., Stovall, T. (2008). *Women Leading Women*, p. 53. Nashville, TN: B&H Publishing Group.

17. Martin, J., Stovall, T. (2008). *Women Leading Women*, p. 52. Nashville, TN: B&H Publishing Group.

18. Martin, J., Stovall, T. (2008). *Women Leading Women*, p.60. Nashville, TN: B&H Publishing Group.

19. Wilkins, J. (December 1, 2016). *Ligonier Ministries*. Retrieved from https://Ligonier.org/learn/articles/mothers-church

20. Moore, Beth. (2019). Twitter, May 6, 2019.

21. Patterson, D., Kelley, R., eds. (2011). *The Women's Evangelical Commentary Old Testament*, p. 374-375. Nashville, TN: B&H Publishing Group.

22. Inrig, G. (1979). *Hearts of Iron, Feet of Clay*, p. 81. Chicago, IL: Moody Press.

23. Wiersbe, W. (1994). *Be Available*, p. 32-44. Wheaton, IL: Victor Books.

Week 4

1. Greear, J.D.(n.d) The Book of Judges: *Right Now Media*. Retrieved from https://www.rightnowmedia.org/Content/Series/257959?episode=4.

2. McGee, J. Vernon. (1983). *Thru the Bible with J. Vernon McGee Volume II*, p.56. Nashville, TN: Thomas Nelson Publishers.

3. Stilley, Lloyd. *Six Trust Lessons from Gideon – Judges 6-7*. Retrieved from https://www.lifeway.com/en/articles/

sermon-gideon-trust-obedience-judges-6-7.

4. Keller, Timothy. (2013). *Judges for You*, p. 67-68. UK: The Good Book Company.

5. Keller, Timothy. (2013). *Judges for You*, p. 69. UK: The Good Book Company.

6. Keller, Timothy. (2013). *Judges for You*, p. 71. UK: The Good Book Company.

7. Keller, Timothy. (2013). *Judges for You*, p. 71. UK: The Good Book Company.

8. Davis, Dale Ralph. (2000). *Judges: Such a Great Salvation*, p. 92. Great Britain: Christian Focus Publications Ltd.

9. Wiersbe, Warren. (1994). *Be Available*, p. 61. Colorado Springs, CO: David C. Cook.

10. Steve Gaines, pastor of Bellevue Baptist Church, Cordova, TN, frequently makes this statement.

11. *Life Application Study Bible*, New Living Translation, p. 486. (2007). Carol Stream, IL: Tyndale House Publishers, Inc.

12. Greear, J.D.(n.d) *Right Now Media*. Retrieved from https://www.rightnowmedia.org/Content/Series/257959?episode=4.

13. *Life Application Study Bible, New Living Translation*, p. 486. (2007). Carol Stream, IL: Tyndale House Publishers, Inc.

14. Davis, Dale Ralph. (2000). *Judges: Such a Great Salvation*, p. 95. Great Britain: Christian Focus Publications Ltd.

15. Wiersbe, Warren. (1994). *Be Available*, p. 65. Colorado Springs, CO: David C. Cook.

16. Davis, Dale Ralph. (2000). *Judges: Such a Great Salvation*, p. 97. Great Britain: Christian Focus Publications Ltd.

17. Keller, Timothy. (2013). *Judges for You*, p. 77. UK: The Good Book Company.

18. Wiersbe, Warren. (1994). *Be Available*, p. 66. Colorado Springs, CO: David C. Cook.

19. Davis, Dale Ralph. (2000). *Judges: Such a Great Salvation*, p. 99. Great Britain: Christian Focus Publications Ltd.

20. Wiersbe, Warren. (1994). *Be Available*, p. 68. Colorado Springs, CO: David C. Cook.

21. Keller, Timothy. (2013). *Judges for You*, p. 77. UK: The Good Book Company.

22. Keller, Timothy. (2013). *Judges for You*, p. 78. UK: The Good Book Company.

23. McGee, J. Vernon. (1983). *Thru the Bible with J. Vernon McGee Vol. II*, p.60. Nashville, TN: Thomas Nelson Publishers.

Week 5

1. Meuller, G. (May 19, 2019). *Daily Inspirations from Great Christians*, Retrieved from https://www.desiringgod.org/messages/george-muellers-strategy-for-sharing-god

2. Lutzer, E. (2018). *The Church In Babylon*, p. 31. Chicago, IL: Moody Publishers.

3. Keller, T. (2013). *Judges for You*, p. 82. UK: The Good Book Company.

4. Smith, J. E. (1995). *The Books of History*, (Judges 6-8:35). Joplin, MO: College Press.

5. Inrig, G. (1979). *Hearts of Iron, Feet of Clay*, p. 131. Chicago, IL: Moody Press.

6. Wiersbe, W. (1994). *Be Available*, p. 44-77. Wheaton, IL: Victor Books.

7. Keller, T. (2013). *Judges for You*, p. 88. UK: The Good Book Company.

8. Keller, T. (2013). *Judges for You*, p. 88. UK: The Good Book Company.

9. Keller, T. (2013). *Judges for You*, p. 87. UK: The Good Book Company.

10. Tozer, A.W. (2004). *Knowledge of the Holy*, p.vii. New York, NY: Harper Collins.

11. Wiersbe, W. W. (1994). *Be Available*, pp. 44-77. Wheaton, IL: Victor Books.

12. Inrig, G. (1979). *Hearts of Iron, Feet of Clay*, p. 135. Chicago, IL: Moody Press.

13. Inrig, G. (1979). *Hearts of Iron, Feet of Clay*, p. 136. Chicago, IL: Moody Press.

14. Keller, T. (2013). *Judges for You*, p. 65. UK: The Good Book Company.

15. Graham, J. (Twitter, May 24, 2019).

16. Inrig, G. (1979). *Hearts of Iron, Feet of Clay*, p. 146. Chicago, IL: Moody Press.

17. Inrig, G. (1979). *Hearts of Iron, Feet of Clay*, p. 147. Chicago, IL: Moody Press.

18. Webb, B. G. (1994). *Judges*. In D. A. Carson, R. T. France, J. A. Motyer, & G. J. Wenham (Eds.), New Bible Commentary: 21st Century Edition, pp. 271-274. Leicester, England; Downers Grove, IL: Inter-Varsity Press.

19. Wiersbe, W. W. (1994). *Be Available*, pp. 44-77. Wheaton, IL: Victor Books.

20. Leeman, J. (Twitter. April 10, 2019).

21. Keller, T. (2013). *Judges for You*, p. 97. UK: The Good Book Company.

22. Smith, J. E. (1995). *The Books of History (Judges 6-8:35)*. Joplin, MO: College Press.

23. Wiersbe, W. W. (1994). *Be Available*, p. 93. Wheaton, IL: Victor Books.

24. Inrig, G. (1979). *Hearts of Iron, Feet of Clay*, p. 153. Chicago, IL: Moody Press.

25. Keller, T. (2009). *Counterfeit Gods*, p. xix. New York, New York: Penguin Books.

26. Keller, T. (2009). *Counterfeit Gods*, p. xx. New York, New York: Penguin Books.

27. DeMoss, N. L. (2004). *Holiness*, p. 75. Chicago, IL: Moody Publishers.

28. DeMoss, N. L. (2004). *Holiness*, p. 131. Chicago, IL: Moody Publishers.

29. Scott, S., Lambert, H., eds. (2012). *Counseling the Hard Cases*, p. 130. Nashville, TN: B&H Publishing.

Week 6

1. Wiersbe, W. (1994). *Be Available*, p. 92. Wheaton, IL: Victor Books.

2. Ingrid, G. (1979). *Hearts of Iron*, Feet of Clay, p. 160. Chicago, IL: Moody Press.

3. Wiersbe, W. (1994). *Be Available*, p. 79. Wheaton, IL: Victor Books.

4. Wiersbe, W. (1994). *Be Available*, p. 80. Wheaton, IL: Victor Books.

5. Wiersbe, W. (1994). *Be Available*, p. 81. Wheaton, IL: Victor Books.

6. Wiersbe, W. (1994). *Be Available*, p.83-84. Wheaton, IL: Victor Books.

7. Wiersbe, W. (1994). *Be Available*, p. 87-88. Wheaton, IL: Victor Books.

8. Wiersbe, W. (1994). Be Available, p. 106. Wheaton, IL: Victor Books.

9. Longfellow, H. (1992) *Retribution: A Spiritual Poem*, p. 81. Boston, MA: Dover Publications, Inc.

10. Keller, T. (2013). *Judges for You*, p.106. UK: The Good Book Company.

Week 7

1. Rainey, D. & Rainey B. (2018). *The Art of Parenting: Aiming Your Child's Heart Toward God, p.* 227. Bloomington, MN: Bethany House Publishing.

2. Calvin, J. (2019). *Commentary on the Book of the Prophet Isaiah Ð Volume II*, p. 286. Translated by A. Uyl. Ontario: Canada: Devoted Publishing.

3. Keller, T. (2013). *Judges for You*, p. 109. UK: The Good Book Company.

4. Keller, T. (2013). *Judges for You*, p. 110. UK: The Good Book Company.

5. Welch, E. (1998). *Blame it on the Brain?*, p. 194. Phillipsburg, NJ: P&R Publishing.

6. Clarke, A. (1970). *Clarke's Commentary, II*, p. 148. NY: Hunt and Eaton.

7. Calvin, J. (2009). *Institutes of the Christian Religion*, p. 55. Peabody, MA: Hendrickson Publishers, Inc.

8. Godin, S. (n.d.). *Stop Stealing Dreams*, p. 60. Free printable edition.

9. Guzik, D. (2003). Study Guide for Judges 11. *Blue Letter Bible*. Retreived from https://www.blueletterbible.org/Comm/archives/guzik_david/StudyGuide_Jdg/Jdg_11.cfm

10. Guzik, D. (2003). Study Guide for Judges 11. *Blue Letter Bible*. Retreived from https://www.blueletterbible.org/Comm/archives/guzik_david/StudyGuide_Jdg/Jdg_11.cfm

11. Tozer, A.W. (2013). *God's Power for Your Life: How the Holy Spirit Transforms You Through God's Word*, p. 33. Grand Rapids, MI: Baker House Publishing.

12. Meyer, F.B. (n.d.). Our Daily Homily. *Precept Austin*. Retrieved from https://www.Preceptaustin.org/judges_devotionals

13. Keller, T. (2013). *Judges for You*, p. 119. UK: The Good Book Company.

14. *Abort73*. (n.d.) Retrieved from https://abort73.com/abortion_facts/us_abortion_statistics/

15. Santayana, G. (1905). *The Life of Reason: Reason in Common Sense*, p. 284. New York, NY: Scribner Publishing.

16. Spiegelberg, N. (1981). *If Only I Had Known*. Retrieved fromhttps://www.godthoughts.com/fanfr.html

17. Shibboleth. *Easton's Bible Dictionary*. Retrieved from https://www.biblestudytools.com/dictionaries/eastons-bible-dictionary/shibboleth.html

18. Deffinbaugh, R.L. (n.d.). *Jephthah: Words Matter*. Retrieved from https://bible.org/seriespage/12-jephthah-words-matter-judges-101-1215

19. Caine, C. (2012). *Undaunted: Daring to Do What God Calls You to Do*, p. 79. Grand Rapids, MI: Zondervan Publishing.

20. Kent, D. G. (1980). *Joshua, Judges, Ruth*, p. 122. Nashville, TN: Broadman Press.

21. *Easton's Bible Dictionary*. (n.d.). Retrieved from https://www.biblegateway.com/resources/eastons-bible-dictionary/Zebulun-Lot

22. Piper, J. (2018). *Don't Waste Your Life*, p. 96. Wheaton, IL: Crossway Books.

23. Piper, J. (2018). *Don't Waste Your Life*, p. 39. Wheaton, IL: Crossway Books.

Week 8

1. Keller, T. (2013). *Judges for You*, p. 134. UK: The Good Book Company.

2. Keller, T. (2013). *Judges for You*, p. 124. UK: The Good Book Company.

3. Keller, T. (2013). *Judges for You*, p. 125. UK: The Good Book Company.

4. Davis, D. R. (2000). *Judges: Such a Great Salvation*, p. 158. Great Britain: Christian Focus Publications Ltd.

5. Wiersbe, W. (1994). *Be Available*, p. 128. Colorado Springs, CO: David C. Cook.

6. Davis, D. R. (1990). *Judges: Such a Great Salvation*, p.162. Great Britain: Christian Focus Publications Ltd.

7. *Life Application Study Bible, New Living Translation*, p.509. (2007). Carol Stream, IL: Tyndale House Publishers, Inc.

8. Keller, T. (2013). *Judges for You*, p. 131. UK: The Good Book Company.

9. Keller, T. (2013). *Judges for You*, p. 131. UK: The Good Book Company.

10. Davis, D. R. (2000). *Judges, Such a Great Salvation*, p. 162. Great Britain: Christian Focus Publications Ltd.

11. Brother Lawrence. (1982). *The Practice of the Presence of God*, p. 34. New Kensington, PA: Whitaker House.

12. Brother Lawrence. (1982). *The Practice of the Presence of God*, p. 32. New Kensington, PA: Whitaker House.

13. Warren, R. (February 16, 2019). *Pastor Rick*. Retrieved from https://pastorrick.com/be-in-constant- communion-with-god/.

14. Rogers, A. (n.d.). *One Place*. https://www.oneplace.com/ministries/love-worth-finding/read/articles/glory-of-gods-presence-11160.html

15. Wiersbe, W. (1994). *Be Available*, p.132. Colorado Springs, CO: David C. Cook.

16. Keller, T. (2013). *Judges for You*, p. 136. UK: The Good Book Company.

17. Davis, D. R. (2000). *Judges: Such a Great Salvation*, p.169. Great Britain: Christian Focus Publications Ltd.

18. Wiersbe, W. (1994). *Be Available*, p. 132. Colorado Springs, CO: David C. Cook.

19. Wiersbe, W. (1994). *Be Available*, p. 133. Colorado Springs, CO: David C. Cook.

Week 9

1. Nielson, K. (2018). *Women and God: Hard Questions, Beautiful Truth*, p. 62. The Good Book Company.

2. Keller, T. (2013). *Judges for You*, p. 146. UK: The Good Book Company.

3. Keller, T. (2013). *Judges for You*, p. 146. UK: The Good Book Company.

4. Walvoord, J. (1973). *The Bible Knowledge Commentary History*, Loc. 2561. Colorado Springs, CO: David C. Cook.

5. Allen, C. (1973). *The Broadman Bible Commentary*, p. 449. Nashville, TN: Broadman Press.

6. Gaines, D. (2017). *Choose Wise, Live Fully*, p.68. Nashville, TN: Abingdon Press.

7. Mainwarin, D.L. (May 27, 2019). *Life Site*. Ex-LGBT men, women rally to show freedom they've found in following Jesus. Retrieved from lifesitenews.com/mobile, news/200-ex-lgbt-men-women-rally-to-show-freedom-they've-found-in-following-Jesus

8. Walvoord, J. (1973). *The Bible Knowledge Commentary History*, Loc. 2590. Colorado Springs, CO: David C. Cook.

9. Packer, J. I., (2018). *Judges: A 12-Week Study*, p.81. Wheaton, IL:Crossway.

10. Keller, T. (2009). *Counterfeit Gods: The Empty Promises of Money, Sex and Power, and the Only Hope That Matters*, p. xviii. New York, New York: Penguin Books.

11. Keller, T. (2009). *Counterfeit Gods: The Empty Promises of Money, Sex and Power, and the Only Hope That Matters*, p. 168-169. New York, New York: Penguin Books.

Week 10

1. Solzhenitsyn, A. (2007). *The Gulag Archipelago Abridged: An Experiment in Literary Investigation*, p. 75. New York, NY: HarperCollins Publishers.

2. Yeats, W.B. (2018). *The Collected Poetry of William Butler Yeats*, p. 145-146. www.digireads.com

3. Wiersbe, W. (2010). *Be Available*, p. 154. Colorado Springs, CO: David C. Cook Publishing.

4. Campbell, D.K. (1989). *Judges: Leaders in Christ Times*, p. 147. Wheaton, IL: Victor Books.

5. Wiersbe, W. (2010). *Be Available*, p. 158. Colorado Springs, CO: David C. Cook Publishing.

6. Peterson, E. (1996). *Living the Message*, p. 74. New York, NY: Harper Collins Publishing.

7. Lewis, C. S. (1974). *The Abolition of Man*, p. 27. New York, NY: Harper Collins Publishing.

8. Campbell, D.K. (1989). *Judges: Leaders in Christ Times*, p. 150. Wheaton, IL: Victor Books.

9. Inrig, G. (1979). *Hearts of Iron, Feet of Clay*, p. 276. Chicago, IL: Moody Press.

10. Piper, J. (2013). *Brothers, We Are Not Professionals: A Plea to Pastors for Radical Ministry, Updated and Expanded Edition*, p. 6. Nashville, TN: B&H Publishing Group.

11. Powlison, D. (2009). "Idols of the Heart and 'Vanity Fair'," *Christian Counseling & Educational Foundation (CCEF)*. Retrieved from http://www.ccef.org/idols-heart-and-vanity-fair

12. Sneed, C. (December 11, 2015). "Stumbling Out Of The Fog:" Memories Of The Worst Traffic Accident in Tennessee History. *Channel Nine News*. Retrieved from http://newschannel9.com/news/local/stumbling-out-of-the-fog-memories-of-the-worst-traffic-accident-in-tennessee-history

13. Inrig, G. (1979). *Hearts of Iron, Feet of Clay*, p. 282. Chicago, IL: Moody Press.

14. *Life Application Bible, New Living Translation*. (2007). Judges 19:1, p. 416. Carol Stream, IL: Tyndale House Publishers, Inc.

15. Harris, J.G., Brown, C.A. & Moore, M.S. (2000). *Joshua, Judges, Ruth*, p. 271. Grand Rapids, MI: Baker Books.

16. McCoy, K. (Twitter. June 3, 2019).

17. Manning, B. (1996). *The Signature of Jesus*, p. 44. New York, NY: Multnomah Publishing.

18. Lewis, C.S. (1996). *Mere Christianity*, p. 103. New York, NY: HarperCollins Publishing.

19. Wiersbe, W. (2010). *Be Available*, p. 170. Colorado Springs, CO: David C. Cook Publishing.19.

20. Keller, T. (2013). *Judges for You*, p. 189. UK: The Good Book Company.

21. Campbell, D.K. (1989). *Judges: Leaders in Christ Times*, p. 163. Wheaton, IL: Victor Books.

22. Tozer, A.W. (1961). *The Knowledge of the Holy*, p 28. New York, NY: HarperCollins Publishing.

23. Inrig, G. (1979). *Hearts of Iron, Feet of Clay*, p. 291. Chicago, IL: Moody Press.

24. Inrig, G. (1979). *Hearts of Iron, Feet of Clay*, p. 290. Chicago, IL: Moody Press.

25. Robinson, R. (1956). *The Baptist Hymnal*, p. 313. Nashville, TN: Convention Press.

26. Robinson, R. (1956). *The Baptist Hymnal*, p. 313. Nashville, TN: Convention Press.

Made in the USA
Lexington, KY
10 September 2019